EDUCATION FOR THE INEVITABLE

EDUCATION FOR THE INEVITABLE

Schooling When the Oil Runs Out

Michael Bassey

Book Guild Publishing
Sussex, England

First published in Great Britain in 2011 by
The Book Guild Ltd
Pavilion View
19 New Road
Brighton, BN1 1UF

Typesetting in Garamond by
Keyboard Services, Luton, Bedfordshire

Printed in Great Britain by
CPI Antony Rowe

A catalogue record for this book is available from
The British Library

ISBN 978 1 84624 639 5

*Dedicated to my grandchildren Sarah, Laura
and Oscar, and their generation*

Contents

Preface

This book represents a confluence of three personal interests: school education, macro-politics and world ecology. 'Wow,' you may say. But when a retired academic like me, who doesn't play golf or bowls but reads the *Guardian* every weekday and the *Observer* on Sunday, broods on these three issues and thinks of his grandchildren and their generation, then it becomes imperative to try to persuade others that urgent actions are needed.

I have lived nearly all of my life in England and belong to the fortunate generation born in the middle years of the twentieth century. I had free education right through to my PhD, free health care through the National Health Service, and now have a teacher's pension and state pension which satisfy my personal needs. In consequence, the ideas on school education in this book are about the English school system – its trials and tribulations due to over-zealous governments since 1988 – and how it could and should be preparing children for the uncertainties of their future. But, sadly, young people in other countries are also bedevilled by their government policies which often, if to a lesser extent, mirror the excessive testing, ruthless inspection and oppressive curriculum control which has become the norm in England. So I hope that readers who share my concerns and who live in other countries will find the criticism of testing, inspection and curriculum control helpful, along with the ideas on collegial schools and bottom-up accountability.

Likewise, the discussion of issues of macro-politics is based on what is happening in England. But my advocacy of the media becoming an educative force, together with the arguments for social justice based on curbs on high pay and the introduction of citizens' income, the discussion of cutting turbo-consumption and developing self-sufficiency, and the encouragement of the promotion of local community development and of international developments on peace, aid and drugs are relevant in every well-developed industrial country that claims to be a democracy. Also, it must be a universal truth that these matters are central to a nation's development of its education system and not, as some may think, peripheral.

While my discussion of school education and macro-politics arises from consideration of the situation in England, the third issue, world ecology, is self-evidently a global matter. Climate change and its consequences in terms of shortages of food and water, and energy shortages in terms of the soon-to-peak supply of oil from fossil sources and the need to cut carbon dioxide emissions, are going to change the lives of people across the world, possibly drastically. On this matter my educational perspective is a universal one, applicable across the world. People need to learn that while growth is how infants move through adolescence to adulthood, once this has been reached further growth is cancerous and destructive. While underdeveloped countries need economic growth and the capitalist values that support it, developed countries should eschew growth, reject the competitive me-first culture and embrace convivial values. In particular, they need to educate their young to comprehend this and give them the skills and understanding which will empower them to create sustainable societies.

Introduction

Upon the Fate of this Country the Education of the People Depends

I grieve at what is happening in education and fear for the future of my grandchildren's generation.

In schools they are being prepared (poorly, I believe) for an economic world that is crumbling and cannot be rebuilt. They are not being made ready to tackle creatively whatever problems (inevitably currently unknown) may arise in their lifetimes. We can hope that they will find ways to establish sustainable ways of living with a reasonable quality of life for themselves and for their successors across the planet. The legacy that we will leave them is much worse than the one we inherited. At least we should ensure that they receive an education that equips them for troubled times.

But education is broader than schooling: it is a lifelong process. While schoolchildren are not being prepared for the problems of tomorrow, their parents and the rest of the adult generation are not learning how today's policies are contributing to problems in the making, and how these might be alleviated.

No one knows when it will happen, or how abruptly, or where it will start, or how harshly it will affect lives, but,

1

inevitably, and probably sooner rather than later, our economic system, essentially based on continuous growth, turbo-consumerism, massive inequality between the greedy rich and the needy poor, and an individualistic me-first culture, will hit the buffers.

In truth, of course, it will probably be the ecological system that hits the buffers, bringing the economic system to a calamitous standstill. It may come from climate change and the consequences of global shortages of food, water and energy. It may come from oil reserves running low and the price of fuel rocketing, with gross consequences for freight, personal transport and domestic heating. This is probably the first major shortage crisis that will hit us. For this reason I use the phrase 'when the oil runs out' as both a likely reality and a metaphor.[1] Alternatively, it may come from the next financial bubble bursting catastrophically and laying waste to jobs, benefits and pensions.

It could come because the hard-working people of the country come to wonder why it is necessary for them to be so 'hard-working' when there is so much wealth around, and they up sticks and demand that we become a 'post-consumer' society. Neal Lawson, chair of the political think tank and activist body Compass, has suggested the merits of such a society:

A society in which children are free to be children, devoid of commercial pressures, where education is about the wonder of learning and opening doors in our minds, where work is creative and fulfilling but there is ample time for family and friends, where the guilt of planetary destruction is lifted from the pit of our stomachs, where we can live in spaces and places that we are free to enjoy and share with others,

---

[1] See the website of the Oil Depletion Analysis Centre, http://www.odac-info.org

where we know each other as equal citizens, and all our lives are valued for the incredible people we are and can be.[2]

Today's politicians fail to tell about the track that we are racing down – they are silent on this, at least in their public pronouncements. Were they to reject economic growth, for example, they fear, no doubt correctly, that they would be derailed long before society reaches the buffers. They clamour for change – different changes according to their different political persuasions – but fail to tell us that massive change is coming irrespective of the politics of today. Others recognise what is happening: the contributors to *Dark Mountain* (2010) for example. The editors, Paul Kingsnorth and Dougald Hine, write:

> Industrial society, after only two centuries, is reaching the limits of its capabilities. From climate change to the emptying of the oceans, from mass extinction to the continuing razing of the forests, we are pushing at the boundaries of the possible and eating away at the heart of the natural world. To imagine that this great engine of taking, which strip-mines the world's riches to manufacture excess for two or three billion people, could do the same for nine or ten billion of us, at the same time as we face a convergence of emergencies ranging from climate change to the peaking of our fossil fuel supplies, is pure fantasy. Windfarms or no windfarms, the world we have known is coming to an end … but this is not the same as the end of the world full stop. The decline or stuttering collapse of a civilisation, a way of life, is not the same as an apocalypse. It is simply a reality of history.

---

[2] Neal Lawson, *All Consuming* (London: Penguin, 2009).

The Dark Mountain Project is not concerned with fantasising about catastrophe; it is concerned with being honest about reality: something which most of us, as human beings, find painfully hard.

When you accept this vision of the future – and it seems that a growing number of people do – then questions inevitably arise: what do we do with our lives? How does this change our choices, and the assumptions on which those choices are made? What kinds of actions still make sense? And, deeper still, there is the question which underpins the Project, what stories do we tell ourselves?

In writing this book, I accept the *Dark Mountain* vision of the future and, after a long career in education involving teaching, teacher training and research, I seek to focus the questions of the above paragraphs onto the future of our children, grandchildren and beyond. This book is the story I tell for them.

My basic premises are:

1. that when the inevitable happens and our ecological system hits the buffers, local communities will become much more significant than they are today and it will be best (if not essential) that young people are educated in the local schools nearest to their homes;

2. that schooling of the young will need to change to equip them for their future. What is taught and how it is taught should be determined collegially by the school in relation to local needs and not centrally by government – hence Ofsted, testing, league tables, and attempts at government micromanagement should end;

3. that these changes will be more acceptable to parents and society at large if every local school is perceived as a 'good' school – which, in terms of social justice, is what every school should be; and

4. that since no one can predict when what I call 'the inevitable' will happen (or how), it is a case of the sooner the better in terms of ensuring that every school is a good school, organised collegially, independent of government, embedded in its local community, with a curriculum embracing nurture, culture and survival, and developing an ethos of conviviality. Yes, it is imperative that we make this a reality now.

But – and this is an essential reservation – reversing the famous utterance of Disraeli of 1874, we need first to understand that upon the fate of this country the education of the people depends. Schooling cannot be changed fundamentally until, first, the voting public, *the electorate*, recognises that it is the ecological predicament, not the economic one, which is the ultimate challenge; until, second, *policy makers* turn our society into one which is more equitable, more just, more democratic and, ultimately, more sustainable; and until third, in order to achieve these changes, *the press* becomes an effective agent of adult education. For this reason, Chapter 1 of this book is not about schooling, it is about political ideas which could change the face and the fate of Britain and prepare it for the uncertainties of the future. Such ideas are essential precursors for creating an education appropriate for coming generations.

1

Truth Must Talk to the People, and the People Talk to Power

As explained in the introduction, this chapter is not about schooling but simply outlines some political ideas which could help create a more just, equitable and democratic society, and thus one in which the educational ideas expressed later in this book stand a chance of succeeding.

The starting point is the need to recognise the dire challenges ahead. Beyond the politics of today, we should have great fear for the future of our children, and their children. This country, and the wider world, will see enormous disruption, if not destruction, of the economic systems on which today's affluence depends. Climate change will lead to humanitarian disasters, and the human consequences of global shortages of food, water and energy will lead to economic turmoil, if not international strife.

To meet these challenges, we need to revitalise the roots of our democracy – liberty, fairness and fraternity – and then add ecology, economy and education.

- LIBERTY: We must protect, not restrict, the freedoms of citizens.
- FAIRNESS: We must tackle the rampant inequalities in our society.

7

- FRATERNITY: We must enhance the notions of the strong protecting the weak, the affluent supporting the poor, the able helping the disabled.
- ECOLOGY: We must ensure that food and energy supplies are planned in the context of expected changes in climate and the need to reduce drastically our carbon footprint. Likewise, we should plan in the expectation of vital resource depletion.
- ECONOMY: We must replace economic growth as a measure of national success by the quality of life of all our citizens. Turbo-consumerism needs to give way to national self-sufficiency.
- EDUCATION: While the policy that every school should be a good school is right, our immediate priority should be adult education to ensure that the challenges facing us are widely recognised, and thus that a balanced national debate can take place about measures the government is taking to tackle them.

So if these are proper aims, how can we advance them? The following political suggestions may seem outlandish at present to many people – but they reflect the gravity of today's challenges, and cohere as a strategy which could lead to a steady state economy, a more equitable distribution of wealth, a fairer and more peaceful world, and a sustainable society for our descendants. These are proper measures for preparing for the inevitable – for the time when the oil runs out. They are changes needed in parallel to a good education for all.

1. Free the media from press barons and see it as an educative force

The media has a vital educative role in a democracy and needs to be more focused on this role. Curiously, while the broadcasting industry of television and radio is regulated – it must give 'balanced coverage' of political issues – newspapers are not so regulated. At present, the privately owned newspapers, in order to maximise sales and therefore profits, entertain their readers with scandals, disasters and crimes and, when giving political news, often colour it with the (usually) right-wing views of their owners or editors. For example, the failings of state schools and teachers are frequently pilloried by certain papers, but their successes rarely profiled.

The thought of condemnatory front-page banner headlines frightens politicians. These three examples of such headlines in the *Daily Mail* make the point:

14 October 2009: OUR WOEFUL SCHOOLS, BY TESCO BOSS

25 November 2009: A LESSON IN INCOMPETENCE – 1 in 3 schools fails to provide adequate teaching; half of academies are substandard; countless start work without 3Rs; £5 billion wasted on adult literacy classes

2 December 2009: A DAMNING INDICTMENT – school spending doubles but GCSE grades barely improve; results at more than half of schools are worse than the previous year; four in ten leave primaries without mastering the 3Rs

All of these statements could be challenged and put into a balanced context revealing that actually most schools are doing well, but what was the message that the 2.1 million people who bought these papers took away about state schools and the teaching profession? That they are rubbish! The fact that many of these problems are associated with economic poverty, over which schools have zero influence, was not mentioned.

A particular concern is that the tabloid papers give their readers extensive coverage of celebrity scandals and sports news but devote little space to significant political news.

Ed Miliband was elected the new leader of the Labour party in 2010. I have researched one of his statements after his election. On 29 September 2010 he said: 'Global warming is the greatest challenge the country faces.'

Should we believe him? Well, when the most eminent scientists in this country say the same, I believe it. In September 2010 the Royal Society published *Climate Change: A Summary of the Science.* It concludes:

> There is strong evidence that changes in greenhouse gas concentrations due to human activity are the dominant cause of the global warming that has taken place over the last half century. This warming trend is expected to continue, as are changes in precipitation over the long term in many regions. Further and more rapid increases in sea level are likely which will have profound implications for coastal communities and ecosystems.

So, come the next election, should Ed Miliband put this as top priority in his party manifesto? Should he put forward drastic measures to curb consumption, cut energy use, reduce carbon dioxide emissions? No. Not yet.

Why not? Because in a democracy, before 'truth speaks to power' it must first speak to the people. The population needs to understand the dangers that will face the nation's children. At present there is vagueness and uncertainty. Between January and March 2010 Ipsos MORI surveyed, on behalf of Cardiff University, a nationally representative quota sample of 1,822 of the British population aged 15 years and older. It found that:

> although the majority (78%) of respondents believe that climate change is happening, the absolute number who believe this has fallen significantly since our last survey (91% in 2005). Similarly, overall levels of concern have fallen since 2005, as have risk perceptions. The current data also show that just under one half (47%) consider climate change to be a product of both human and natural activities, while just under one third (31%) consider climate change to be mostly or entirely a man-made phenomenon.

Clearly there is a significant gap between scientific evidence and public opinion. And so I ask, to what extent do newspapers try to close this gap?

How do people learn about what's happening in the world? Television and personal chit-chat – yes. But also nearly ten million of us buy one of the nine national weekday newspapers. What do they say about climate change and global warming? And, beyond the aim of increasing circulation and making profits for their owners, do they carry a responsible message about 'the greatest challenge the country faces'?

I conducted a survey of our nine national daily newspapers over recent years up to the beginning of October 2010. It is as though they are printed on different planets. Here are my findings:

- *The Sun* (circulation = 3 million; owner: Rupert Murdoch) – gives its readers occasional news of disastrous climatic events that experts suggest may be due to global warming.

The paper has a bias towards accepting that global warming is happening, but there is no in-depth discussion of the causes or how to tackle them. Pithy headlines and plenty of humour.

- *Daily Mail* (circulation = 2.1 million; owners: heirs of Lord Rothermere) – until August 2010 its news items were sceptical, and its articles in denial, of global warming. Suddenly its editorial policy has changed to acceptance of the scientific evidence.
- *Daily Mirror* (circulation = 1.2 million; owners: Trinity Mirror plc) – occasional news items on global warming. Bias towards accepting scientific evidence.
- *Daily Star* (circulation = 0.8 million; owner: Richard Desmond) – in between the pictures of glamorous celebs in various states of undress there are some powerful brief reports on global warming featuring experts and sceptics.
- *Daily Telegraph* (circulation = 0.7 million; owners: Barclay brothers) – scepticism nearly all the time. Staff reporter James Delingpole spreads his denial of global warming – but Met Office warnings get published.
- *Daily Express* (circulation = 0.7 million; owner: Richard Desmond) – the best read for those in total denial! Especially 15 December 2009 on '100 reasons why global warming is natural'.
- *The Times* (circulation = 0.5 million; owner: Rupert Murdoch) – tends to publish more sceptical news than items on 'orthodox' global warming.
- *The Guardian* (circulation = 0.3 million; owner: Scott Trust) – no pussyfooting. The editorial staff and key columnists see global warming as fact and present substantial articles on it and its likely consequences.
- *The Independent* (circulation = 0.2 million; owner: Alexander Lebedev) – has been vociferous about global warming, but

on 10 September 2010: 'Global warming? It doesn't exist, says Ryanair boss O'Leary'.

In a world which has dire challenges ahead, newspapers have a vital educative role. One paper stands out in this respect: the *Guardian* and its Sunday sister, the *Observer*. They regularly give readers detailed news reports and informative articles on the likely dangers ahead. Why is this? Perhaps it is because they do not have an owner seeking maximum profit and have an ethos of responsibility to the community.

The Guardian Media Group (GMP) is owned by the Scott Trust. As its website explains:

> this is a unique form of media ownership in the UK: unlike others the GMP does not seek profit for the financial benefit of an owner or shareholders, but [aims] to sustain journalism that is free from commercial or political interference, and uphold a set of values laid down by C P Scott, the great *Manchester Guardian* editor.

These values are honesty, integrity, courage, fairness, and a sense of duty to the reader and the community.

Since newspapers are a significant vehicle of adult education, surely all newspapers should have high-minded aims and values? Perhaps it is time for them to forsake the profit-making rationale (while ensuring financial stability, of course) and, in their different styles, to find a way of balancing celebrity culture and sports news and comment with sufficient political, social, economic and ecological news and comment to enable the reading public to know what grave challenges face the world – and what Parliament and the government are, or should be, doing about them.

Our government should find democratic ways of limiting the

power of press moguls, perhaps by insisting on ownership being in the hands of trusts with publicly enunciated aims and requiring trust members to be resident citizens. Balanced political adult education should be one of those aims. It is an essential precursor to the introduction of the ideas that follow in this book.

2. Justice demands curbs on high pay

The book *The Spirit Level: Why More Equal Societies Almost Always Do Better*, by R. Wilkinson and K. Pickett,[1] shows that inequality in the UK is higher than in many other industrial countries around the world and that inequality correlates with many social and environmental problems, such as ill health, lack of community life, violence, drugs, obesity, mental illness, long working hours and big prison populations. So, how can we reduce inequality in our society?

One answer is for a maximum take-home pay as an agreed and universal multiple of a living minimum wage. Before the very rich squeal too loud, we should ask whether it is the gross income that gives them the craved esteem of their fellows, or the take-home income. The fact is that prestigious salaries and bonuses are quoted as gross, and not after tax as net. So, if this is the testosterone of the higher echelons of the business world, let them be paid these gross sums, glory at the level, boast about it, but pay tax which reduces it to the chosen national maximum! Provided, of course, that the tax authorities can track them down and ensure that people who claim citizenship, make their money here, use our infrastructure, and enjoy our national culture pay their taxes here in full.

---

[1] R. Wilkinson and K. Pickett, *The Spirit Level: Why More Equal Societies Almost Always Do Better* (London: Allen Lane, 2009); see also D. Dorling, *Injustice: Why Social Inequality Persists* (Bristol: Polity Press, 2010).

It is noteworthy that the Tory/Lib-Dem coalition talked at one time of introducing a maximum wage for people in the public sector, but dared not suggest the same thing for the business world! Michael Gove, Secretary for Education, said that no head teacher should earn more than the Prime Minister (whose salary is £142,500). This is nearly 14 times the minimum wage. (He was shouted down on this proposal.)

Since the strong evidence is that low achievement in education is more prevalent where there is poverty, we can expect that measures to reduce economic inequality in our society will be found to support the raising of school standards.

3. Citizen's income

This is an idea which has been around for a long time. Citizen's income would be paid to everybody as the right of a citizen in our advanced and prosperous society, and not be means tested. It would replace state pensions, child benefits, most disabled benefits, tax credits and unemployment benefits. The last of these will be vital at a time of economic turbulence when many jobs are lost and new ones (hopefully in green industries) slowly come into existence. But it would be recouped in tax from everyone in paid employment, and for this reason would be administered by the Inland Revenue. It would entail higher taxes for the better off, and fits neatly with the concept of a maximum take-home wage.

Citizen's income would lift the household income of impoverished homes. Thus it would begin to resolve many of our social and environmental problems and would provide the basis for an economic system sustainable into the distant future. It is in accord with the principles of fraternity and fairness. Set at an appropriate level, citizen's income linked to a maximum take-home pay would be such that across the nation more people would gain than would lose. So it should be possible to enact such changes in a democracy – provided that the media gives a balanced account of how it would work.

4. 'Business as usual' is not an option – we need to cut consumption

Lord Stern made the first point very clearly in his major report on climate change, yet many industries, and especially the financial ones in the City of London, have chosen to ignore this warning. Neal Lawson, in *All Consuming*, refers to

> a consumer industrial complex of marketers, advertisers, media moguls, designers, retailers, psychologists, analysts, share traders, transporters, growers and producers with an insatiable appetite for more [as] they strive to sell us more, to win a greater share of the market, to grow their profits, boost their share price so that they earn more and we buy more.

It is this turbo-consumerism that we need to find ways to curb. Lawson argues that there are two interlinked ways of doing this:

> First, we can make decisions to buy differently and to buy less. Individual action empowers and enlightens us and lots of small changes can make a big difference. But as well as change from the bottom of society we need change from the top. We need a critical mass of people to act and can't assume that they will without support

and awareness that everyone else is playing their part. We need laws and regulations that help create a post-consumer society.

There are two major reasons for curbing consumerism. First, the planet cannot sustain the present levels of consumption of the industrial countries, which are a major contributor to global warming. Yet the poorer nations of the world, seeing our levels of consumption on worldwide television, seek the same. Second, consumerism in the industrial countries has reached levels at which those of us with money to spend have many possessions, but are not happier as a result. Consuming has become too much a way of life. Lawson again:

> If we want a good life, then we need hours and days when we refuse to or can't buy things. The choice to go on choosing has to be taken away. It is time to walk, sit, stare, cycle, daydream, watch clouds, rivers or the sea, jog, go to public buildings, read in the library, volunteer, fly a kite, contemplate in a church or listen to the band in the local park. We can do so much that we really enjoy without having to shop.

Consumerism is the handmaiden of economic growth. Neither is appropriate for the future. There are economists who understand this, and we need them to guide the policies of government. To those who say that economic growth is the only route to reducing poverty we must say that there is a better answer, and one that, unlike failed trickle-down theory, should work: it is redistribution of income through a curb on high pay and establishment of citizen's income. It is quality of life for all that matters, not affluence for some and poverty for others.

Again the media has a vital role here. The problem, of

course, is that our newspapers depend upon advertising, and advertising is about persuading people to consume. This is not the place to 'sort out' the newspaper industry, other than to recognise that when the oil runs out major changes will be needed. Could it be that not-for-profit newspapers serving an educative role (among others) deserve some support from taxation?

5. Self-sufficiency in food and energy

In a troubled world our future will be more secure if we grow more of our own food. Suppose, for example, that we set a target of producing 90 per cent of our own food within ten years. There would be many implications for the farming community, food manufacturers, food distributors and supermarkets. A related idea is to ensure that every family where the breadwinners are out of work has the opportunity of using an allotment for growing vegetables and fruit. In dense urban areas this may require careful organisation.

In terms of energy we need to recognise that while we need to reduce our carbon dioxide emissions drastically, it is likely that in the near future global oil production will peak and liquid fuels will become increasingly expensive. This will have major implications for international freight and for personal travel. This becomes an argument for localising food production and, in terms of personal travel, trying to develop local communities and bicycle travel. There can be little doubt that we need to reduce our energy consumption and actively develop energy sources utilising wind, wave and solar power.

Developing self-sufficiency in food and energy will mean that many jobs will be lost and new ones created. This is why the idea of citizen's income is important, because it will ensure that people are supported in the gap, which may be long, between one job and the next.

6. Community development

In the past, communities were the strength of the nation, providing support for young, old and infirm people and companionship for all. In the twentieth century, for a variety of reasons, including cheap travel, home amusements of television and computer games, migration to urban centres for work opportunities, and lurid media stories of crime and murder, many communities were weakened and people became more wary of those living near to them.

In the near future, when rocketing oil prices make transport more expensive, people will necessarily be more localised. With many people living longer lives there will be increasing demands for support for the elderly, and already we are finding that local authorities are over-stretched. These are good reasons for rekindling community spirit.

We need to aid community development. If every school is a good school, parents will be prepared to send their children to the local school – and this is a potent force for community development. If local libraries are well stocked and local sport centres and community centres well equipped, people will use them. If allotments are available, people will often share them – and give surplus crops to their neighbours.

One national venture that has been particularly successful was the Big Lunch, initiated by the Eden Project. Encouraging the organisation of community street parties on a Sunday in the middle of July, it was launched in 2009 with these words:

A day when, for a few glorious hours, cars will stop,

shyness will stop, gloom will stop and Britain will come together in the street to meet, greet, share, swap, sing, play and laugh for no reason other than we all need to.

Perhaps this Sunday should be declared a national holiday – with shops and everything except essential services closed for the day: the Big Lunch Holiday.

7. International policies – peace, aid and drugs

One of the roots of democracy cited earlier is fraternity. In preparing for the future we need to look closely at the way in which we relate to the rest of the world and, in particular, how we – the affluent – support the poor of the world. A difficult issue is that we know that the poor of the world can never reach our level of affluence and, while many of them may want to achieve it, we also know that our level of affluence is becoming self-destructing. What we may hope is that people everywhere can achieve an acceptable quality of life consonant with their historical development, cultural norms and territorial resources. The top priority must be world peace – an absence of strife – followed by humanitarian aid.

First, we should support international efforts to end the arms trade. The export of weapons from this country should be banned outright. Too often our weapons are used for aggression, not defence. Yes, it will cost jobs, but these can be remade if our death factories begin to 'turn swords into ploughshares' and manufacture and export simple farming equipment, water pumps and hand tools.

Second, our military policies need to be reconsidered. We should renounce all nuclear and biological weapons on both moral and practical grounds and support others in doing the same. We should recognise that we can only rarely stop some of the awful crimes committed against humanity around the world by military force. But where we are reasonably sure that we can achieve humanitarian ends, we should be sure that our soldiers are properly equipped, and if they come home wounded, that we give them every support they need, and if they don't come home (as every soldier knows is a possibility), that we support their families.

Third is international aid. In terms of the Millennium Declaration, of which our country was a co-signee, we must continue to provide financial aid to the governments of poor countries and, when possible, increase it. Likewise, because climate change (for which, in part, we are responsible) is likely to lead to an increase in humanitarian disasters around the world, we must be ready to provide rapid aid. But, put simply, we need to ensure that our support enhances the lot of the impoverished and doesn't line the pockets of the powerful. It may be that every aid package should come with a plane-full of anti-corruption accountants and lawyers.

Fourth, we should work internationally to decriminalise the drug trade. Prohibition policies have failed. Careful legislation is required to regulate the supply and quality of narcotics and to support programmes for ending addiction. Apart from releasing police resources, reducing the prison population and improving public health in this country, it will help reduce strife in countries like Colombia and Afghanistan.

Why are these points relevant to future schooling? They are essential because moral education is a fundamental part of the upbringing of the young. Yet any parent or teacher developing ideas of what is right and what is wrong cannot escape the shadows on the wall – the arms trade, our military incursions, our low contributions to aiding the poor of the world, and our ambivalence over narcotics.

None of the tasks outlined here would be easy, but they are all designed for creating a future for our children based on the tenets set out earlier: liberty, fairness, fraternity, ecology, economy and education. Of course, they require our politicians to step outside the boxes of tribal politics and strive for the good of a future which is, obviously, unknowable.

Unknowable? Yes – but not unpredictable. There are many natural scientists, social scientists and writers who have deep insights into where we are heading and, to return to the first task, they need to contribute regularly to an enlightened media. There used to be an academic slogan that said, 'Truth must talk to power.' A better version would be: 'Truth must talk to the people, and the people talk to power.' That is democracy. And it is the essential precursor to every school becoming a good local school.

2

Education Based on Nurture, Culture and Survival

Education, education, education...!

In a less hurried and more thoughtful world it would be valuable for all who make policies on education first to be clear on what they mean by education, and second, to make public their meaning. In today's public discussions, the concept of 'education' seems to be used as though we all give it the same meaning and know what that is.

When Tony Blair became Prime Minister in 1997 and announced his policy of 'Education, education, education', it was seen as a good sound bite, but what did he mean by those three words?

- Was it that young people should acquire useful knowledge and technical skills in order that they could become affluent adults and so contribute to the future gross domestic product?
- Was it that they should develop human values which would help them grow personally and socially as good people?
- Was it to support their nascent creativity, develop their

23

aesthetic values and immerse them in the culture of their time?

- Was it that they might gain a love of learning and the intellectual skills to acquire knowledge and become lifelong learners?

In contrast, a castaway on a fertile island might see education as learning to get food and build shelter; a primitive community might see it as helping the next generation to do the same.

On those rare occasions when politicians give voice to the purposes of education they usually focus on the first of these – the economic argument, with perhaps a glance at the second – the moral argument. The cultural focus[1] features in discussions of curriculum, but the idea of lifelong learning is often ignored, as is any consideration of education for survival. The evidence is that politicians are little interested in the purposes of education, but obsessive about tinkering with its structure and mechanics in the belief that changes will enhance the country's future economic growth.

Since I reject the idea of the necessity of economic growth, as noted in the previous chapter, it follows that I do not see that as a reason for changing the way our schools are organised. I have a different rationale for change. But, first, how should we perceive education?

---

[1] Politicians like to have their say. When Alan Johnson was Secretary of State for Education (in 2007), he wanted teenagers to read Jane Austen and Charles Dickens and, at the time of writing (2010), Michael Gove in the same office wants the poetry of Pope and Shelley to be at the heart of classroom teaching and for every pupil to learn 'narrative British history'.

A framework definition based on nurture and culture

With trepidation, some years ago I set out a *framework* definition of education, and with minor modifications, have used it in a number of writings. It drew on the work of M.V.C. Jeffreys – in a book entitled *Glaucon: An Enquiry into the Aims of Education* (1950) – and included the concept of the 'worthwhile' as used by R.S. Peters in *Ethics and Education* (1966), to focus on 'worthwhile living' and 'worthwhile culture'. I leave the description of these terms to the individual, community, or national government to determine – and hence call it a 'framework', because it provides a structure within which people can put their own constructions. To my surprise, over the years nobody has challenged it. This is how I expressed it until recently:

> Education is: first, the experience and nurture of personal and social development towards *worthwhile living*; and second, the acquisition, development, transmission, discovery, conservation, and renewal of *worthwhile culture*.

This framework embraces the educational activities of *learners* (experience, acquisition, development), of *parents* and *teachers* (nurture, development, transmission), of *scholars* and *librarians* (conservation), and of *artists, scientists, engineers, politicians, pioneers* and *researchers* (discovery, development, renewal); but it doesn't give individual meanings to the notions of worthwhile living and worthwhile culture.

Two examples illustrate these concepts. The introduction of the National Curriculum in England and Wales in 1988 and its subsequent modifications were massive attempts by government to define what shall be transmitted to children in schools as worthwhile culture. Likewise, the mission statements, pastoral

25

policies and codes of behaviour which all schools in England and Wales have been required to develop since the early 1990s are local definitions, devised by governors and teachers, of what constitutes, for them, worthwhile living.

But what about education for survival?

Recently I came to realise that something is missing from my framework definition. Like most people living in the comfort of twenty-first-century English society, I forgot that survival is the first law of the jungle. It is, of course, this which leads us to teach young children the Green Cross Code for crossing the road and to caution them about other dangers at home or in their wider locality.

But the dangers for tomorrow's adults will be much greater than those of their present childhood. As noted in the introduction, our 'comfortable', protected society is fragile. There are many potential dangers: the oil is running out; global warming with climate change, a rise in sea levels and land inundation is happening; nuclear war, biological war, uncontrollable plague could strike; famine and drought are badly affecting some parts of the world; some key mineral resources are becoming exhausted; industrial pollution may be causing sterility and other malfunctions of the human body; and perhaps other, presently unknown, dangers are around the corner.

As a result of this realisation I have added a third item to my definition: embracing education for survival.

Education is about nurture, culture and survival

My framework definition embraces education in nurseries, primary schools, secondary schools, colleges, universities, the home life of families, and the workplace. In short, it includes all of an individual's life-learning from birth to death.

Every individual experiences education throughout their life and through a variety of modes of learning. These include: being nurtured and developing values; acquiring skills and know-how; creating and developing ideas and artefacts; gaining knowledge from family, friends, teachers, authors, poets, artists, musicians, journalists and others; researching and discovering new concepts; conserving and treasuring artefacts; thinking and renewing ideas; talking, listening, debating, arguing; and there are no doubt others.

These modes of learning come together in this definition:

First: education is the experience and nurture of personal and social development towards worthwhile living; second: education is the acquisition, creation, development, transmission, conservation, discovery, and renewal of worthwhile culture; and third: education is the acquisition, development, transmission, conservation, discovery, and renewal of skills for worthwhile survival.

This is a framework which provides a structure on which to locate ideas on what is 'worthwhile'.

Worthwhile living

'Worthwhile living' embraces notions like social relationships with others, personal satisfactions and one's sense of place and purpose in the world.

As an example, my view of worthwhile living is based on the concept of conviviality. This is a way of living through which people gain quality of life and enjoy happiness by striving to be in harmony with themselves and with their social, cultural and natural environments. For each individual this can be a lifelong learning project: I believe for every society it can be a source of peace, prosperity and sustainability. It is an idea developed in Chapter 8.

Others take a different view of worthwhile living, seeking quality of life and happiness by acquiring and spending wealth, and recognising personal ambition and competitiveness as the driving forces needed to achieve these. This is, in effect, the capitalist view.

Worthwhile culture

What do we mean by 'culture'? I find helpful the views of Jon Hawkes, an Australian planner, set out in *The Fourth Pillar of Sustainability: Culture's Essential Role in Public Planning*, published in 2001:

> Culture is the bedrock of society: the tangible and intangible manifestations of our values and aspirations; our customs, faiths and conventions; our codes of manners, dress, cuisine, language; our literature; our arts, sciences, technologies; our history and geography; our sports, pastimes and hobbies; our religions and rituals; our norms and regulations of behaviour; our traditions; and our institutions of groups of humans.

Somehow, from this enormous canvas, tradition has carved out those elements that have been deemed worthwhile and therefore worthy to be taught in school. More recently, government has taken over this role by defining a national curriculum, but one hugely influenced by tradition.

Worthwhile survival

But what of the third element – worthwhile survival? In terms of safety in the home and on the roads, this has obviously been a prime concern of parents and child-minders. Likewise, schools endeavour to teach safety measures in both the classroom and the playground – even if sometimes they become obsessive, such as where playing conkers or throwing snowballs has been banned.

Geography lessons today include global warming and the dangers of climate change. But there is a big gap between becoming aware of these dangers and taking individual action in terms of cutting back on consumption, conserving energy and recycling waste.

Education for creating sustainable ways of living requires major changes in the school curriculum. When our society hits the ecological buffers, such an education will become paramount. I believe it should start now. This is discussed further in Chapter 9.

Who decides what is worthwhile?

The question that my definition poses is: what is it that determines the 'worthwhile'? Is it a matter of tradition, meaning that our predecessors decided it for us? Or is it one of government edict? This might seem to be a democratic answer, but actually means that a group of government-sponsored self-styled experts are empowered to legislate on what teachers must do in the thousands of schools across the country. Or is it one of decisions made by individual schools in relation to their own values of what is 'worthwhile'?

My firm answer is that such decisions should be made by

the teachers and governors of collegial schools (see Chapter 4) after careful consideration of traditional practices, local needs, government-sponsored guidelines and any other suggestions that come to hand. It places great responsibility and fundamental trust on teachers and governors, and that is right. It is why teachers in their training need a thorough grounding in what philosophers have said about education, and also in educational history, and why governors need to be balanced members of local society.

3

Parents Know Differently From What the Press Tells

Parents' views of their children's schools and of other schools in 2010

In the second week of March 2010, a national and representative sample of 1,211 people were interviewed face to face in their homes by Ipsos MORI on behalf of the trade unions NASUWT and Unison. Among other questions, they were asked how good or how poor schools are.

A fascinating difference was revealed in the answers. Of the 230 parents with school-aged children (5–16 years old), 40% said that the *schools their children attend* are 'very good'. Of the 981 respondents without children in this age range, 19% thought that the *schools attended by the children of their immediate friends and neighbours* were 'very good'. But when both groups (1,211 respondents in all) were asked how good or poor they thought the standard of *state-funded schools across England* was, only 8% gave them the accolade of 'very good'.

Combining the results for 'very good' and 'fairly good', of those with their own children in school 79% described their school/s this way. On this measure, friends' and neighbours' schools scored 65% and the nation's schools 54%. At the other

31

end of the scale, combining the results for 'very poor' and 'fairly poor', only 9% of parents said 'yes' to these descriptions, and those without children at school thought the same about their friends' and neighbours' schools. But looking at the nation's schools overall, 19% of those in the two groups thought that they were 'fairly poor' or 'very poor'. The results are set out in Table 1.

Table 1. Perceptions of how 'good' or 'poor' schools are (Ipsos MORI poll March 2010)

	Overall, how good or poor do you think the school/s your children attend are? (N = 230)	Overall, how good or poor do you think the schools attended by the children of your immediate friends and neighbours are? (N = 981)	Overall, how good or poor do you think the standard of state-funded schools in England is? (N = 230 + 981 = 1211)
Very good	40%	19%	8%
Fairly good	39%	46%	46%
Neither good nor poor	8%	13%	21%
Fairly poor	6%	7%	16%
Very poor	3%	2%	3%
Don't know or can't say	4%	13%	7%

Press views of schools in 2010

What is particularly interesting is to see these findings in relation to some of the things that the national press had been saying in the weeks prior to the questioning in March 2010.

The *Sun* told its readers on 25 February: 'Education in Britain is in a terrible state after nearly 13 years of Labour meddling.' The *Star* said on 14 January that GSCE students had been 'failed by Labour': 'half of all the pupils fail to get five decent grades'. The *Daily Mail* on 1 January reported: 'Government spending on schools soars but parents are flocking to go private.'

It would seem that most parents, knowing that they are satisfied with their own schools, presume that it must be elsewhere that the rot is. But even then they reckon that things aren't as dire as the papers tell them. Perhaps they realise that press gloom is endemic to newspapers. These are headline quotes from the nine national daily newspapers in England over the ten months up to October 2010:

The Sun: 'Education in Britain is in a terrible state after nearly 13 years of Labour meddling', 'One in 3 schools not good enough', '1 in 5 kids fail exam in English', 'Generation exam blow: more than 340,000 kids last year failed to get five good GCSEs including English and Maths'.

Daily Mail: 'One in six boys can't write their own name by the age of five', 'One in six pupils are behind in three Rs when they leave primary school', 'Return to real lessons: Dickens and key dates in history to be taught to raise standards', 'A lesson in incompetence: How 1 in 3 schools fails to provide adequate teaching'.

Daily Mirror: 'Unruly pupils cost each teacher half an hour a day', 'One in six pupils are falling behind in English or maths by the time they leave primary school, official figures showed', 'Half of special needs kids just need better teachers', 'Schools "must act on poor teachers"', '47% of schools "not good enough"'.

The Star: 'UK primary school class sizes biggest in developed world', 'Almost half of schools in England are not giving pupils a good education, inspectors said', 'GCSE students "failed by Labour": half of all the pupils fail to get five decent grades.', 'UK bottom of student numbers table: fewer people are entering education compared with other developed nations', 'School exams data to be published … amid growing concerns about school leavers' skills', 'Tesco chief raps "woeful" education: employers are left to bear the brunt of "woefully low" school standards'.

Daily Telegraph: 'appalling indictment of the state school system', 'bad behaviour in schools', 'schools exaggerating special needs to hide poor teaching', 'poor state schools', 'pupil behaviour "poor in fifth of schools"', 'our schools turn out unemployable blockheads'.

Daily Express: 'Sats results: 35% of 11-year-olds fail reading, writing and maths', 'MORE than a third of children leave primary school unable to read because teachers want to entertain them rather than instruct', 'Pupils in nearly half of all schools in England are not getting a good enough education, inspectors said', 'Labour failed on schools', 'Superheads to take over hundreds of failing schools', 'Labour shame as "inadequate" schools double', 'Labour's schools failure makes parents weep: many 11-year-olds won't be going where they had hoped in September'.

The Times: 'Half of schools failing to provide a "good enough" education', 'Must do better and cheaper: education put to the test', 'Challenges for our education system. We cannot hope to be economically competitive in an increasingly globalised world unless we solve some of the structural and cultural problems in our education system', 'Education: the high fly, the rest sink. And no one acts', 'Tesco boss criticises UK education system', 'Poor education standards "are not caused by poverty"'.

The Guardian: 'They can't read, can't write, keep time or be tidy: Tesco director's verdict on school-leavers', 'As many as half of the children identified as having a category of special educational needs (SEN) are wrongly diagnosed and simply need better teaching or pastoral care instead, a report says', 'Half of schools "not good", say inspectors', 'one-in-seven secondary schools inspected by Ofsted in England last term were branded "inadequate"'.

The Independent: 'More than 700,000 pupils wrongly classed as having "special needs"', 'A sickness in our schools: the debate about examination standards', 'One in seven secondary schools branded inadequate: Ofsted admitted it had raised the bar', 'If kids can't read or count, how do they get a job?', 'Sir Stuart Rose told the CBI conference that school leavers "were not fit for work" – they "can't do reading, can't do arithmetic and can't do writing". The minister for schools, on the other hand, says kids are "better equipped than ever" for the world of work'.

'Shock-horror' sells newspapers (or so the editors think), but not all agree

Newspapers, of course, tend to print 'shock-horror' stories more often than 'praise and glory' ones. Presumably it is perceived by their editors as a way of encouraging sales. Most of the press is right wing and so, when Labour is in power, it can be expected that any failings in schools will be used to attack the record of the government. Sats results, GCSE results and Ofsted reports all provide opportunities for headlines to say '35% fail' rather than '65% succeed'. When business people bemoan the lack of skills of some job applicants the press can turn it into a major story and give the impression to newspaper readers that illiteracy is widespread and, moreover, that it must be the fault of teachers and government. It is heartening to see that the *Independent* quoted the minister for schools saying that young people are 'better equipped than ever', up against the CBI speaker saying that they 'were not fit for work'. In a House of Commons debate in January 2010, Vernon Coaker, Minister for Schools in the Labour government, was quoted in Hansard thus:

> We should start every debate by praising our head teachers, teachers and schools for the excellent work they have done and for raising standards in our country. [Interruption.] I bet the Opposition Members who are shouting at me now do not go back to their constituencies and say to their schools that standards have fallen.

The simple statistic from GCSE results that the percentage of students gaining 5 GCSEs at A*-C has risen from 33% in 1989 to 69% in 2009 is clear evidence of what has been achieved.

International evidence: 2006

In March 2006 Harris International, an American pollster using an online survey technique, polled adults in the UK, Germany and Spain. A report[1] by Mike Baker, BBC News education correspondent, points out that people in Britain (with or without children in school) have a higher opinion of education standards than those in the other two countries, and that people directly involved in education as parents tend to be 'more satisfied with the reality they see every day of the week than those who base their views on second-hand information'. The poll results were as shown in Table 2.

Table 2. Satisfaction with school standards: Britain, Spain and Germany (Harris poll, 2006)

	Satisfied with standards at their child's school	Satisfied with standards generally at state schools
Britain (N = 2,114 adults)	64%	42%
Spain (N = 1,136 adults)	44%	31%
Germany (N = 1,309 adults)	36%	22%

Opinion polls can be misleading,[2] but, from reputable pollsters who describe their sampling and identify any sponsor, they can be valuable indications, for better or worse, of where public opinion stands.

---

[1] *BBC News*, 17 March 2006.
[2] Ben Goldacre, in the *Guardian*, 20 November 2010, describes what he calls 'a master class' in leading poll questions towards getting the answers that the poll sponsor seeks. He showed that 6 in 10 people living near to Hinkley nuclear power station supported it being expanded. People are easily manipulated!

What is wanted of a school by parents and public in general?

In March 2009 Ipsos MORI conducted a poll of just over 1,000 English parents on behalf of the magazine *Prospect*, and Amelia Hill reported on the findings in the *Observer*.

Almost all these parents said that manners and good behaviour are vital lessons that schools should teach children. Most agreed that full and stable levels of staffing were essential to a good education, and 74% wanted a good library. Interestingly, only 64% of these parents 'rated good overall academic results as the defining feature of an ideal school'. The survey found that most parents wanted their children to be educated in a broad mix of abilities, cultures and background – in mixed-sex, mixed-race classrooms. Fewer than 1 in 6 believed that selecting pupils on the basis of their religious faith or gender was a key element in a good school. It seems that what most of these parents are looking for is simply a good comprehensive secondary school and a good primary school counterpart.

One other poll by Ipsos MORI, carried out at about the same time, is worth mentioning. It's part of an ongoing garnering of public opinion on ideas of the 'ideal society'. The following was said to interviewees: 'People have different views about the ideal society. Please tell me which of the following statements comes closest to your ideal.' One pair of these statements is given in Table 3, and is relevant to this chapter. It was asked in 1989 and again in 2006.

Table 3. What the public wants of schools (Ipsos MORI polls in 1989 and in 2006)

Statements	2–13 March 1989 (N = 1,458 GB adults aged 15+)	12–17 January 2006 (N=1,001 GB adults aged 18+)
'A country in which the schools provide children with a wide-ranging general education'	61%	68%
'A country in which the schools provide children with the particular skills and attitudes wanted by employers today'	33%	29%
No opinion	6%	3%

It is a question that deserves being asked of a larger sample and then analysed in terms of parents and non-parents, as well as of social class, occupation, and age of the respondents. The answers can, of course, be interpreted as calls for political action or, alternatively, as calls for public education!

4

Everybody Wants a Good School – But What is *a Good School?*

A 'good' school is one that provides the best education for each and every one of its young people. It is where the pupils and the teachers are happily and purposefully working together, where the parents have confidence in the teachers and respect them, and where the local community sees the school as an integral part of a vibrant society. It embraces a curriculum and a pedagogy that responds effectively to the needs and aspirations of its pupils. It is a place where achievements are high because young people choose to study hard, are taught well by their teachers, are encouraged by their parents, and are influenced by a positive climate towards school work by their peer group of class-mates.

We can imagine that those 40% of parents in the Ipsos MORI poll described in the previous chapter who consider the schools their children attend to be 'very good' would subscribe wholeheartedly to the description in the above paragraph. But the others, to varying degrees, would be saying, 'OK, but how do our schools become like this?'

It is not an easy question to answer. If it were, then the government would by now have turned round the schools which they label as 'failing' or 'unsatisfactory'. Unfortunately, governments have tried to improve the weaker schools by narrow testing of pupils, by ruthless inspections, by league tables and the naming and shaming of struggling schools in the daft expectation that competition and market forces would act to either lift the standard of the weak or close them down. It may have raised the game of some schools, but it has damaged the sense of providing an all-round education in many others.

There are, I believe, six conditions needed for all schools throughout the country to be deemed 'good schools'. These are:

(1) that the school has good teachers who work collegially;
(2) that the school has good governors who actively support the school;
(3) that the school has a good regional administration which supports all of the schools within its jurisdiction;
(4) that the school has ready access to ideas flowing from professional bodies, universities, and a National Education Council about educational progress;
(5) that the school receives adequate funding from central government; and
(6) that accountability for progress and expenditure is assessed not by testing or inspection, but by a process starting with school self-evaluation, and working though governing bodies to local administrations to a National Education Council to Parliament and hence to the general public.

These ideas need elaboration. Number 6 in this list is discussed in Chapter 7. The rest are discussed below.

Good schools need to be collegial

Just over one hundred years ago, in 1905, the Board of Education declared in its handbook – aptly called *Suggestions for the Consideration of Teachers* – that:

> each teacher shall think for himself, and work out for himself such methods of teaching as may use his powers to the best advantage and be best suited to the particular needs and conditions of the school. Uniformity in details of practice (except in the mere routine of school management) is not desirable, even if it were attainable. But freedom implies a corresponding responsibility in its use.[1]

Teachers usually worked on their own. They chose their own teaching methods. In primary schools the only external influence on the curriculum was the 11+ tests in English and mathematics. In secondary schools, university requirements on matriculation and the general schools certificate (GSC) examinations in the grammar schools and, later, the general certificate of secondary education (GCSE) in all secondary schools, influenced what was taught, particularly during the fourth and fifth years. The more demanding requirements of higher schools certificate and then A levels determined very largely what was taught in the sixth form. Nevertheless teachers tended to work in isolation of each other, with their own teaching methods and own slant on the required curriculum. They prepared and gave their lessons and maintained discipline (or failed to) on their own.

In the hands of the best teachers this model provided an excellent education, allowing full opportunity to use their

---

[1] Quoted by Colin Richards, professor and former HMI, in a *Times Educational Supplement* article, 21 April 2006.

creativity, insights and enthusiasm. But because of its autonomous nature, it isolated the weaker teachers and deprived them of both the criticism and the support they needed in order to improve their practice. And worse, it tended to protect any incompetence on the spurious grounds that it would be unprofessional for other teachers to interfere. Each teacher could shut the classroom door and say to the world, 'Keep out.' Only the very occasional HMI inspection – or forceful head teacher – could push open that door.

The 1988 Education Reform Act was a justifiable assault on the idea of the autonomous teacher. The idea that the individual sense of responsibility of each teacher was sufficient to ensure that behind the closed classroom door pupils were getting the best possible education was no longer tenable. Unfortunately, in the years following 1988, government ministers and government-appointed agencies became more and more prescriptive in their determination to raise standards in schools. The external testing of pupils and the inspection of teachers and schools became perceived by many as instruments of persecution and so began to damage what governments were trying to improve.

The autonomous teachers who were 'thinking for themselves' were replaced in effect by 'knowledge-and-skills technicians' working to the government's manual and rule book! Teachers lost the opportunity for spontaneity, creativity and educational insight that had characterised the work of the best in the profession, but the work of the weaker teachers certainly improved in a transformation in which 'diamonds were dimmed and pebbles polished'.

Schools were forced to move from one extreme to the other, neither extreme giving all young people the best education in the widest sense. What is needed is for *schools*, not *individual teachers*, to have autonomy while having ready access to the best advice.

And so we come to the idea of the *collegial teacher* working in a collegial school where the classroom doors are, metaphorically if not literally, open. In a collegial school, teachers work as colleagues, sharing responsibility for what happens throughout the school. They are not autonomous agents. In collegial schools it is the teachers who determine the curriculum, the pedagogy, and the assessment of pupils, not national or local government.

These are the major features of a collegial school:

1. The school's overriding aim is to provide for the best all-round educational experience of each and every pupil; this entails:
   - teachers striving for all pupils, as far as possible individually, and especially for those with special needs:
     o to master the basic skills needed for their school work and their adult life (communication, reading, writing, simple mathematics, and basic IT);
     o to develop their emotional sensitivity and personal morality;
     o to be nurtured in their development of survival and social skills;
     o to be appropriately immersed in the culture of their time;
     o to develop their cognitive, creative and physical talents towards achieving their potential;
     o to enjoy their years of schooling; and
     o to eventually leave secondary school with such certificates and documents as demonstrate their personal achievements;
   - teachers working collegially, supporting each other and regularly evaluating the work of the school;
   - mutual respect between pupils, teachers and parents;

- ordered calm which is conducive to learning;
- parents and pupil being regularly informed of, and having opportunities to discuss, the educational progress of the pupil;
- the buildings, equipment and grounds of the school being appropriate for these attributes;
- the funding of the school being directed carefully and intelligently towards these attributes, and
- the school being recognised by the local community as a 'good' school, meaning a place where their young are well educated in the terms described above.

2. Decisions as to the most appropriate curriculum for the pupils are taken by the staff of the school and involve parents and governors; they draw on published research evidence and professional guidance, and share ideas with neighbouring schools, in order to identify and provide the best education for their pupils.

3. Colleagues recognise the strengths and weaknesses of each other and draw encouragement from the first and give support to the second.

4. Assessment for learning has become part of the day-to-day practice of every teacher.

5. Assessment of attainment is made from time to time (perhaps once a term) by the teachers themselves and is communicated to parents.

6. The head and any deputies are recognised as the educational leaders of the school in leading the development of the pedagogy, the curriculum and the assessment of the school, and in challenging and supporting the work of individual teachers.

7. Parents are regularly in touch with the educational development of their children.

8. The governors, seen as lay representatives of the parents and of the local community, are included in the educational discussions of the school and can, from time to time, give the local administration an accountability report on the extent to which the school is achieving its stated aim.
9. The teachers enjoy the trust of parents and the respect of society at large.
10. The school gates are open to parents and the local community, but closed to national government and its agencies.

Collegial schools will be very much more effective at providing every child with a worthwhile education than today's government-controlled schools dominated by fiat, inspection and testing. Likewise, they will be far more effective than those schools of the mid-twentieth century where each teacher was autonomous and the school lacked cohesion. Freed of government control, collegial schools will permit the professional commitment, experience and training of the teachers to flourish, while being accountable to the local community through the school governors for the effective education of their pupils.

Critics may say that this asks too much of teachers and, to the extent that at present teacher training does not prepare them for this total responsibility, this may be a valid point. (This is discussed further in Chapter 11.) But it does not have to be introduced overnight. Freeing schools from government control and regulation does not prohibit them from continuing teaching the way they have in recent years, but it permits them to develop collegial ways of working at their own pace.

Good schools need good governors

Like everything else in the education system, and perhaps elsewhere, the role of school governors has become increasingly complicated and demanding. The UK government Department for Education, which keeps changing its name, has poured out instruction after instruction to school governors. According to a Ministerial Working Group report entitled 'The 21st Century School: Implications and Challenges for Governing Bodies', governing bodies now have 85 functions! Apparently there are 300,000 school governors in England, with 11 per cent of posts vacant, with vacancies particularly evident in inner-city areas. It notes the following as a key finding: 'The majority of governing bodies do a good job.' This is not the place to analyse the statutory functions or delineate the problems that have arisen in some schools between governors (lay volunteers) and school staff (professionals). But it would be interesting to see how schools fared before these 85 functions were introduced. How many of them are really necessary?

These are the six functions which I believe should be the responsibility of school governors:

- discuss termly reports from head about educational work and progress of the school;
- visit classrooms, talk to teachers, parents and others about work of the school;
- challenge and support the school staff when, as lay people, they deem it necessary;
- have oversight of the school's expenditure (through their finance committee) and ensure that it is properly audited;
- work with the head teacher in the appointment and dismissal of staff;
- work with the head teacher to prepare an annual report

to the local administration. Thus, governors play a central role in accountability.

These six functions would seem to be a sensible definition of the essential role of lay volunteers in contributing to the work of a school. They are what good governors should do. The notion in current legislation that governors should set the ethos, aims and objectives of a school is plain daft. These should properly be the decisions of the head and teaching staff, working collegially – which, as shown above, includes discussions with governors as representatives of the local community.

How do the governors come into office? I suggest that they should be elected by the local community (perhaps at the same time as parish councillors).

Good schools need good local administrations

National governments, both Labour and Conservative, have denigrated local authorities (until recently known as local education authorities [LEAs]). National government regularly implies that local government is exercising too much control over schools. Since the introduction in 1988 of local management of schools – whereby schools became primarily responsible for their financial spending (but not their income) – and the National Curriculum, this criticism has become unjust. But it is true that while some LEAs have been highly supportive of schools within their jurisdiction, others have not. This is not the place to pursue these arguments. But what is worthwhile is to identify the functions a good school requires an external body to carry out in order to support the work of the school and to ensure that appropriate funds are channelled from national government to school.

In my view, the following are the proper functions of local administrations:

- to draw up catchment areas[1] for the primary and secondary schools within its area with proper respect for the sensitivities of local communities;
- to carry out regular censuses of numbers of pupils and, of these, the number with particular special needs, in order to inform national government of the local requirements for revenue funding;
- to carry out regular censuses of school buildings and sites in order to assess aspects which require revenue funding from national government above the norm;
- to ensure that sufficient school places are available for the local population by advising national government when extensions and repairs to existing schools or the building of new ones are needed;
- to transfer revenue funds from national government to schools following national formulae (i.e. for salaries, equipment, materials, maintenance, etc.);
- to ensure that national government makes such additional revenue payments as may be needed for pupils with special needs, specialised resources, and specific site issues for particular schools, following national guidelines;
- to support the financial administration of smaller schools (which are too small to employ a financial administrator) and to arrange for the audit of the accounts of all schools and colleges to provide financial accountability;
- to support the governing functions of schools through employing a limited number of inspectors/advisors who,

---

[1] The argument for catchment areas is put in the next chapter.

50

in particular, will scrutinise (giving both challenge and support) reports of governing bodies;

- to collate reports from school and college governing bodies and to forward these to a National Education Council,[1] with a brief commentary by the administration;
- to have at least one member participating with governing bodies in the appointment of new head teachers;
- to maintain one or more offices and appropriate staff to carry out these duties.

With the exception of the first item, these are all administrative functions, not tasks demanding authority; for this reason, I would prefer them to be named 'local education administrations'. Perhaps they should be quite removed from the work of elected county and borough councillors, since their functions are essentially administrative, and the locus for new educational initiatives consists of the schools themselves. Perhaps such local education administrations need to be based on larger areas than those of the present authorities.

Good schools need access to good ideas

Schools should not function in isolation. As noted above, decisions as to the most appropriate curriculum and pedagogy for the pupils should be taken by the staff of the school. This would be a task of daunting responsibility if teachers were starting it from scratch. But they are not. At present all schools have a curriculum in operation – determined in part by central government and in part by inheritance of what has gone before.

---

[1] The notion of a National Education Council, a body independent of government but funded by it, is discussed in Chapter 7.

Once freed from government control, schools can continue to operate as before, and slowly and deliberately reframe their curriculum through discussions with parents and governors, by drawing on published research evidence and professional guidance, and sharing ideas with neighbouring schools. Hopefully, once established, the National Education Council will begin to provide areas for research evidence to focus on, and through its biannual reports to Parliament show how different areas of the country are tackling the curriculum.

Good schools need adequate funding from central government

Ultimately it is a state education system that we are looking at. The state has, rightly, assumed responsibility for the education of the nation's children. Parents are required by the state to ensure that their children attend school (or are otherwise properly educated).[1] Schools are funded by the state. Teachers' salaries are paid by the state. (The notion that school governors in different localities should decide to pay their teachers on different scales in order to attract the best is totally alien.) Schools are built and maintained by the state. Classrooms are equipped by the state.

The 1988 Education Reform Act made a valuable change in the financing of schools by giving schools a budget and requiring head teachers and governors to administer that budget. It meant that decisions about numbers of staff, the purchase of equipment, and the renovation of classrooms were taken by the schools themselves, and, with a healthy increase in funding over the next twenty years, substantial improvements in the

---

[1] Of course, as is well known, while 93% of our children are in state schools, the other 7% are in independent schools financed by the fees paid by their parents. While many of these schools may claim to be 'good schools', within my definition, they are not included in the discussion in this section. Here we are talking about state-funded schools.

nature of schools took place. How far the cost-cutting measures of the present Coalition government will negate these gains remains to be seen.

In the 1990s it was said that only two people in the Department of Education knew how the national school grant system through which local authorities funded schools was calculated – and one of them was due to retire! Since then it has become even more complicated, with the appearance of special funds for the pet schemes of here-today-and-gone-tomorrow education ministers, and with national grants being supplemented by local authorities to different extents. According to a 2008 research paper from the Institute for Fiscal Studies (IFS) by Chowdry, Muriel and Sibieta, 'Despite undergoing significant reform in recent years, the system of state school funding in England remains opaque and poorly understood.'

Nevertheless, this IFS research team has persevered, and its paper in March 2010 entitled 'The Pupil Premium: Assessing the Options' gives a valuable account of how schools are currently funded. It reports that the funding per pupil in primary schools varies between £3,000 and £6,000, and in secondary schools between £4,000 and £7,000. Funding is highly skewed towards schools with greater numbers of pupils with special education needs (SEN), particularly if those pupils have statements, and towards schools with greater numbers from deprived backgrounds.

That schools with greater numbers of pupils with special needs should get extra funding in order to provide extra support for them is clearly right. But it has long seemed unjust that secondary schools should get greater funding than primary schools.[1] From a national perspective it can be argued that it

---

[1] As long ago as 1994 the House of Commons Select Committee on Education pointed this out as unjust.

is unjust that local authorities augment the income from central government from their council tax revenues to widely different extents.

In terms of justice, irrespective of postcode it is right for the national government to have a funding rate per child going directly to schools, *and for this to be augmented by additional funding* for children with special needs and for particular school circumstances (for example, split sites, small schools, problematic buildings). This is a complex issue beyond the scope of this book, but I mention it because it demonstrates the need for local data collection – which I have suggested might be done by newly created local educational administrations.

If every school were a good school, then most parents would choose the local school. But how can parents, the local community and the nation be assured that the local school *is* a 'good' school? Ensuring that this is the case should be the role of school governors, using self-evaluation by the school, and reporting to local community and local education authority, who in turn should report to a National Education Council and through that to Parliament. This is discussed in Chapter 7.

The role of the state should be to provide sufficient funds and, within the structures described in this chapter and the accountability measures set out in Chapter 7, to trust the teachers, the governors and the local community to spend taxpayers' money responsibly and wisely.

A 'good' school grows from the inside, not from the outside. Government edicts, Ofsted inspections, examination pressures and league tables do not create 'good' schools. A 'good' school is such because of the combined efforts of teachers, pupils, parents and school governors, and as such deserves the public trust.

In these terms, parents should be happy for their children to attend the local school – which, as is argued in this book, will become inevitable 'when the oil runs out'.

5

Choice of School – A Political Chimera[1]

Police cars, fire engines, ambulances, schools and cornflakes

'Is that the emergency switchboard? Police, please. My house has been burgled.'

'There are three police forces you can approach. Press * and then 1 on your telephone keypad for the latest statistics of their success rates in catching burglars. Then press # and key in the number for your chosen force.'

'Emergency switchboard? Fire brigade please. My house is on fire.'

'Press * and 2 on your telephone keypad for the response-time statistics of the nearest fire brigades in your area...'

'Emergency – I need an ambulance quickly please...'

'It sounds like you have a burst appendix. Do you want to go to the nearest hospital or to the one in the fifty-mile range with the lowest post-operative infection rate?'

Choice is not a universal good. In an emergency we want quick action, not the opportunity of choice. On the other hand, in

---

[1] Wikipedia's definition of 'Chimera': 'a monstrous creature with parts from multiple animals'.

deciding what breakfast cereal to buy, or where to go on holiday, or which house to live in, we value having a wide choice.

Now, when a particular brand of cornflakes or muesli is popular and the shelf is getting depleted, the store quickly orders more from its wholesaler. In a well-managed store, favourite brands never run out. But what happens when parents come to choose a school?

Catchment areas

Before the 1988 Education Reform Act there were catchment areas for schools, and when a child reached age 5, and later age 11, the local education authority would tell the parents which school their child should go to. At age 5 it would be the *local* primary school; at age 11 either the *local* comprehensive school or, in areas with an 11+ exam, the *nearest* secondary modern school or grammar school, according to how the child performed. The 1988 Act opened up a market in school choice. While schools still have catchment areas, which may help in the decision as to who should attend when there are more applicants for places than places in the school, parents are free to choose which schools they will apply to for admission for their children.

I live on the outskirts of Newark, a market town of 27,000 inhabitants. Putting my postcode into the 'Find schools' search facility of the government's website,[1] I learn that there are, within a mile and a half of home, three state primary schools, and two secondary schools within five miles. Only one of the primary schools is within easy walking distance (a third of a mile), and I would need to be a brave (or foolhardy) parent

---

[1] http://www.schoolsfinder.direct.gov.uk/

to allow an 11-year-old to cycle to either secondary school (both a mile and three-quarters away) along our busy local roads.

Fifteen years ago we lived in the Nottinghamshire village of Kirklington, and there was but one primary school within a mile and a half of home (quarter of a mile from us), and one secondary school (three miles from us) within a five-mile range (with a school bus provided).

By contrast, my daughter lives in a south London borough where there are nineteen primary schools and three secondary schools within one mile of their home which my grandchildren might attend. This illustrates a significant difference between rural, suburban and metropolitan areas. Outside the metropolitan areas there is very little choice – or none – except for parents who have the time and money to run a taxi service for their children.

So what happens when a school gets more applicants than it has places for? In a sense, instead of children (or their parents) choosing the school, the school chooses the children. Legislation prohibits selection by ability (except for the 164 grammar schools dotted around the country), and so each school has its own admission procedure, which, for a church school, may involve parents' religious affiliation, and for most schools may in some way involve distance from home to school. So, in a sense, there are still catchment areas operating when demand for school places exceeds supply.

Governments of both the left and the right have encouraged choice

Governments, both Conservative and Labour, have encouraged parents to choose the schools at which they want their children to be educated. Parents are encouraged to look at league tables of results – of Sats for primary schools, and of GCSEs and A levels for secondary schools – as well as at Ofsted inspection reports and school prospectuses, and if they can, to visit the schools. But unlike supermarkets, schools cannot readily provide extra places to meet demand, and in the event, in 2010, over the country as a whole, one family in ten did not gain their first-choice primary school, and one in six did not gain their first-choice secondary school. In inner-city areas the situation was worse in terms of parents not getting their first choice schools.

Choice is a political mantra popular with politicians. It rarely seems to be thought through. Yet it should be self-evident that if Ofsted and exam results put one school above others, then most of the parents who weigh up the evidence will choose that school. Schools cannot expand at short notice and so, inevitably, many parents are going to be disappointed. And these parents may vote against the politicians who encouraged them to have high hopes. The idea that this choice will operate, via market forces, to raise the standards of all the schools seems crazy: it may work for cornflakes, but it will not work for schools.

The choice must eventually be the local school – but it must be a good school.

As many have said to the deaf ears of government and would-be government, it isn't a choice of schools that is wanted for children, it is a local good school where they are taught by skilled and committed professionals, work with congenial classmates and have ample opportunities to develop both as all-rounders and wherever their individual talents may lie.

When the inevitable happens and our ecological system hits the buffers, the first basic message in my introduction to this book is that it will be best if children are educated in local schools nearest to their homes.

In order that everybody can countenance this, the message is simple: as discussed in the previous chapter, all schools should be good schools. That requires ample numbers of good teachers and support staff who give continuity to their work place and who are valued and respected by the public at large, and given adequate funding.

The current political approach – 'good schools will be enlarged, bad ones closed' – is inept. Closure of schools takes time and causes distress to the children involved and damage to the local community. Non-local schooling breaks up communities – children don't meet their neighbourhood mates, and opportunities for their parents to meet other local parents are reduced. And the wider environment suffers from the resulting increase in vehicular travel to and from school.

Political ambitions at the cost of educational ideals

Why is it that our political leaders are putting the emphasis on parents' choice and claiming that this is a means of raising standards of education? The most likely explanation is that 'we will let you choose' is seen as a vote-catching slogan. Any opinion poll that asks, 'Do you think parents should have a choice of schools?' will only get 'No' answers from people who have understood and agreed with the arguments set out above. Otherwise they will think that, like cornflakes, choice is a good idea. The divisive nature of parental choice, leading to sink schools on the one hand and elite schools on the other, is only of concern to those who understand the issue.

The weaknesses of some schools may be due to some of the professionals who teach at them, but more commonly it is due to the inequalities in our society. Poverty destroys hope and aspiration; it leads to apathy and lethargy. Where there is widespread unemployment, parents' disillusion results in their children having little incentive for school learning. Offering parents a choice of schools is not a way to help neighbourhoods that are struggling with poverty. Tackling poverty is the starting point for raising the game of struggling schools, which is why some of the measures put forward in Chapter 1, seemingly having nothing to do with education, are actually important for these schools.

That parents want a choice of school for their children is natural and understandable. Obviously they want the best for them. But once they can be assured that every school is a good school, they should be content for their children to attend whatever the local school is.

Governments of the left and the right have argued that offering parents a choice of different types of schools (trust, specialist, faith, academy, free, etc.), the firm hand of Ofsted, the league tables of test and exam results, the defining of the National Curriculum, and the endless flow of directives from the Department of Education are all aimed at producing 'good' schools. These are not, however, the way to reform the system. What government has not understood is that a 'good' school grows from the inside, not as a result of pressure from the outside.

Re-introduction of firm geographical catchment areas

Insisting on children attending their local school will require the re-introduction of firm geographical catchment policies, as was the case before the 1988 Education Reform Act. For parents who have been encouraged to exercise choice, this will be seen as a draconian measure. It may be that not until the price of personal travel becomes exorbitant – when the oil begins to run out – will parents be willing to accept the idea. Children walking to and from their primary schools and walking or cycling to their secondary schools will be healthy for them and save their parents both money and time in terms of ferrying them in cars. But first, as stressed earlier, every school must carry the accolade of being a good school. Once league tables are abolished it will be easier for the importance of this to be recognised.

How can 'sink' schools turn into 'good' schools?

There are no easy answers. If there were, we can be sure government would already have resolved the issue. But it is a question that cannot be shirked.

Suppose that every local administration set up a small group to examine the problems of each 'struggling' school. Perhaps it would comprise the head, with a couple of governors of the school, a couple of the teaching staff, a couple of parents, a head from a nearby 'successful' school, and, as chairperson, a significant public person from the locality (an MP, a county councillor, or a magistrate, for example). The brief would be to find why the school is 'struggling' and to suggest ways of raising the levels of achievement. This investigating group should take evidence from every teacher and every governor, in either written or oral form.

First they should try to ascertain whether the existing staff, including the head, are of the calibre found elsewhere in successful schools.[1] Then they should ask: 'What is the measure being used to describe these schools as "struggling"?' If it is

---

[1] Yes - the head would be present at a meeting to decide whether he or she's got what it takes. Why not?

Key Stage 2 (KS2) assessment results in a primary school, they should ask questions like: 'Are there many children for whom English is not their first language?' 'Is the level of home poverty such that the adults are too depressed to take interest in their children's schooling?' 'Are there too many children with special educational needs that the existing staff is not qualified to tackle?' They might move on to questions that consider whether there are alternative indications of success, like 'Do the children seem happy in school?' 'Are they lively and outgoing?' 'Do they try to work hard or is there a sub-culture of anti-school among the children?' 'To what extent do the parents support the school?' Then come the questions as to what support would help. 'If the children, or some of them, spend another year in the school and transfer to secondary school at 12 rather than 11, might this raise the level of their reading, writing and number work to the "expected" Level Four of the National Curriculum in teacher assessments?' 'Are extra staff needed to reduce class sizes and so aid classroom teachers, or are specialist staff needed to deal with some of the children with special educational needs?' 'Are extra funds needed to improve the physical state of the school buildings and so, hopefully, raise the morale of everybody working there?'

Similar questions and actions should be carried out in struggling secondary schools. In this case, it will be poor GCSE results that lead to the school being seen as 'struggling'. It might be appropriate to ask whether too many students arrive without having achieved Level 4 in reading, writing and maths, and whether this seriously affects their studies. If there is much unemployment among the parents, how far does this lead to students seeing working for GCSEs as futile, 'because there are no jobs here anyway'? To what extent are unemployed parents offered voluntary work in the school?

In each case, the chair should write a straightforward report to the local administration and put it in the public domain on a local website, and hopefully also have it printed in a local newspaper. A public meeting might be called to muster support for the measures put forward. Schools should campaign for success.

'Good' schools grow from the inside

Why hasn't this been done before on a national basis? When Labour introduced academies, it was moving in this direction by putting substantial funds into school buildings, but instead of putting the initiative in the hands of the schools, it decided that business executives should show the schools how they should be run. As various research reports have shown, sometimes this approach has worked and sometimes not. Now the Conservative/Lib-Dem coalition has introduced a Pupil Premium, which is to be paid to schools with students from poor families, in order to help them raise the standard of achievement. It is a modest payment and, again, is a top-down initiative and not something from the grass roots of the schools.

What governments have not understood is that a 'good' school grows from the inside, not the outside, as I have stressed in the previous chapter. It is the commitment and ideas of the teachers, the leadership of the head teacher, the enthusiasm for learning of the pupils, the support of parents, governors and the local community that determine its success – not the extent of government initiatives. Government's role should be to channel appropriate amounts of taxpayers' money into ensuring that all of the schools that taxpayers' children attend are deemed 'good'.[1]

---

[1] Thank goodness few of the taxpayers without children have ever objected to this. Retrospectively, of course, they were funded by taxpayers when they went to school – unless they were of that small minority educated at independent schools.

The choice for secondary students should be the local comprehensive school

In Chapter 10 I argue the case for rethinking secondary education around the question of: what should a good local comprehensive school do? This presupposes that grammar schools and faith schools will be turned into such. A few words in defence of this proposition are in order.

In England there are 164 grammar schools among 3,200 secondary schools. According to a poll carried out in March 2010 for the National Grammar Schools Association, 70% of people questioned supported the retention of these grammar schools and 76% supported the introduction of more. It shows that there is not wide understanding of the argument that the existence of grammar schools (creaming off the more able students at age 11) means that, for the rest, in their locality they only have secondary modern schools (which are deprived of the most talented youngsters), and so the social and academic advantages of comprehensive schools are lost. Come the need for local schools, the grammar schools will have to become comprehensive.

Faith schools

Faith schools go back to 1902, when there was an agreement between the government and the Church of England and Roman Catholic Church leaders which established the system of voluntary aided and controlled church schools. A few Jewish schools were established during the twentieth century, and recently Islamic schools have been formed. Public concern has been expressed in some quarters about some of the latter teaching an Islamic fundamentalism which could threaten the social cohesion of the next generation, while other worries have been expressed about Christian fundamentalism in the form of creationism being taught in some of the new academies.

A 2009 research study from the Institute of Education, University of London (by R. Allen and A. Vignoles) tracked 550,000 students in state secondary schools in order to examine the impact of faith schools on neighbouring schools and on social stratification. Contrary to a theoretical possibility that competition might raise standards all round, they found that faith schools did not improve educational standards in other local schools. It did, however, in the localities studied, promote social divisiveness.

Significantly the Christian think tank Ekklesia, the British Humanist Association, and a senior Jewish Rabbi have all expressed concern about the impact of these schools. Their coalition, Accord (which includes the teaching union ATL [the Association of Teachers and Lecturers]), has commented as follows, drawing on the Institute of Education's research report:

Despite a steep decline in church attendance across all denominations and limited support for the principle of state-funded religious schooling in attitude surveys, there continues to be relatively high demand for places at religious secondary schools. On a typical Sunday in 2005, just six per cent of the population attended church, with under two per cent in Anglican or Catholic churches. Yet 15 per cent of children are educated in religious secondary schools. In 2005, 64 per cent of respondents agreed with this statement in an ICM poll: 'Schools should be for everyone regardless of religion and the government should not be funding faith schools of any kind'.

Religious secondary schools have an impact on all other schools in the area. Some parents are more likely to choose faith schools than others. Socio-economically advantaged pupils and high achieving pupils are more likely to be enrolled in faith schools.

This research considers whether areas with high numbers of faith school places have higher levels of academic achievement and/or higher levels of social and ability segregation across schools.

Overall, the results suggest little positive effect on education standards from the competition effect exerted by faith schools. Education standards in areas with high numbers of faith school places are no better than elsewhere. But social and ability divisions across schools are worse in areas with a large number of faith schools.

The chair of Accord, Rabbi Dr Jonathan Romain, said:

It is a sad situation when children are 'sorted' into schools according to the beliefs and socio-econometric status of their parents. This research shows that areas with a high proportion of religious secondary schools educate children no better, but divide them far more.

When every school is a local school, the status of faith schools will need to change.

Independent schools

While I am clear that grammar schools, faith schools and every other kind of state-funded secondary school will have, 'when the oil runs out', to become good local comprehensive schools (as discussed in Chapter 10), it is unlikely that fee-paying schools, independent of state funds, could be drawn into the same system. But what I envisage will happen to them is that, with a maximum wage established, there will be fewer parents able to pay the substantial fees of private education, and when they recognise that the comprehensive schools are good places of education, those who would previously have opted for fee-paying schools will decide to send their children to the local comprehensive school instead. Thus the independent schools will slowly wither – and the social mix of the comprehensive schools will benefit.

The menace of estate agents and house moving

At present estate agents tend to cite good Ofsted reports or high positions in league tables as selling points for houses in the vicinity of successful schools. It must be hoped that when every school is recognised as a good school this practice will wither. Likewise, the anxiety of parents which leads some to seek homes located near successful schools should eventually disappear. It will take time, but it will be in accord with the political ambition, expressed in Chapter 1, that we become a more equal society, with a narrowing of the gap between rich and poor.

Evidence from the United States

Diane Ravitch, author of *The Death and Life of the Great American School System* (2010), spent many years as an education administrator (at one time she was Assistant Secretary of Education in the federal government), and now is passionately sceptical of practices that she once supported. Of neighbourhood schools she writes:

Do we need neighborhood schools? I believe we do. The neighborhood school is the place where parents meet to share concerns about their children and the place where they learn the practice of democracy. They create a sense of community among strangers. As we lose neighborhood public schools, we lose the one local institution where people congregate and mobilize to solve local problems, where individuals learn to speak up and debate and engage in democratic give-and-take with their neighbors. For more than a century, they have been an essential element of our democratic institutions. We abandon them at our peril.

Business leaders like the idea of turning the schools into a marketplace where the consumer is king. But the problem with the marketplace is that it dissolves communities and replaces then with consumers. Going to school is not the same as going shopping. Parents should not be burdened with locating a suitable school for their child. They should be able to take their child to the neighborhood public school as a matter of course and expect that it has well-educated teachers and a sound educational program. (pp. 220–221)

I agree!

It is worrying to see how her description of accountability based on simplistic test scores, of schools excluding low achievers in order to score high, of principals being sacked for not raising test scores, of school curricula in one area focusing on reading and maths for five hours a day in high school, and of business people pushing performance pay to get results in schools, is a description of something that happens across the Atlantic and yet influences our politicians. As another American, David

Berliner, of Arizona University asks in the foreword to a recent English account (*Reinventing School, Reforming Teaching: From Political Visions to Classroom Reality*, by John Bangs, John MacBeath and Maurice Galton, 2011):

> How can bad policy be formulated by so many, for so long, over successive governments? If we are ever to learn how to improve schools and enhance the profession of teaching we must look at the mistakes of the past ... and learn lessons from them.

6

Goodbye to Government Control: Time to Wield Occam's Razor

In Chapter 4 I described a good school as one where all-round achievements are high because young people choose to study hard, are taught well by their teachers, are encouraged by their parents, and are influenced by a positive climate towards school work by their peer group of classmates.

Ever since the 1970s, politicians of both the left and the right, in and out of government, have been trying to find ways of turning all schools into 'good' schools – albeit with varying definitions of what this might mean. Today we have a national curriculum; Ofsted inspections; Sats, GCSEs and A-level league tables; a plethora of information from the government to enable parents to choose schools; and a constant flow of edicts to schools from the government on how to improve their work. All have been introduced to try and improve our schools, and for the same reason we have a bewildering variety of school designations – in the public sector, there are community schools, foundation schools, trust schools, faith schools, voluntary-aided and voluntary-controlled schools, city technology colleges, specialist schools, academies, and now Michael Gove's 'free' schools; and in the private sector, there are independent, private and public schools. Wow!

This complexity is mind-blowing for parents seeking to do the best for their children. Yet it is unnecessary. What matters is what happens between pupil and teacher. There are many ways of expressing this. The poet Kahlil Gibran, in *The Prophet*, put it like this:

> If the teacher is indeed wise he does not bid you enter the house of his wisdom, but rather leads you to the threshold of your own mind.

It is time that politicians left the business of teaching to those who, by commitment, training and experience, are best able to decide what happens in classrooms – the teachers themselves. It is they who are nearest to knowing where lies the 'threshold of the mind' of their pupils.

The one Education Act that Parliament should enact is one which abolishes the National Curriculum, Ofsted, Sats and league tables, and sweeps away the labels and external controlling bodies of schools to bring them all under one umbrella of state-funded, collegially operating, local schools where the teachers are trusted to decide what is best for their pupils, are committed to striving to the best of their ability to provide it, and are strongly supported by school governors and the local community, within the accountability framework described in the next chapter.

Politics and schools 1944–2010

It is instructive to see how politicians have tried to improve schools. In 1944 the Butler Education Act tidied up previous legislation and introduced secondary education for all in terms of the tripartite system of grammar, technical and modern schools. One clause is particularly relevant to the ideas of this book:

> ...it shall be the duty of the local education authority for every area, so far as their powers extend, to continue towards the spiritual, mental and physical developments of the community...

Today I would replace the words 'local education authority' with 'local school'.

In 1965, when Tony Crosland was Secretary of State, Circular 10/65 requested local authorities to submit proposals for reorganising their schools as comprehensives, and in the same year the Certificate of Secondary Education (CSE) was introduced to provide a qualification lower than the General Certificate of Education (GCE) at O level. In 1986 these two were replaced by the General Certificate of Secondary Education (GCSE). These were major structural attempts to improve the nation's school system.

Earlier, in October 1974, Keith Joseph, as Conservative shadow Home Secretary, made a much publicised speech on a perceived decline in national life, that he attributed in part to the education system. Brian Simon, educational historian,[1] described Joseph, in his call for a 'remoralisation' of national life, as saying this:

> Values were being systematically undermined. Parents were being diverted from their duty as regards education, health, morality, advice and guidance. Delinquency, truancy, vandalism, hooliganism, illiteracy – all these accompanied

---

[1] Brian Simon, *Education and the Social Order: 1940–1990* (London: Lawrence and Wishart, 1991).

the decline in educational standards... Particular venom was directed at 'left-wing intellectuals', motivated primarily 'by hatred of their own country'. In a powerful climax Joseph claimed that 'these well-orchestrated sneers' from their strongholds in the educational system and media 'have weakened the national will to transmit to future generations those values, standards and aspirations which have made England admired the world over'.

The floodgates were open. *The Times*, the *Guardian* and the *Daily Telegraph* gave space to assaults on comprehensive schools. BBC's *Panorama* screened a damning programme of a day in a 'typical' comprehensive school (unfairly choosing a social priority school), and Cox and Rhodes Boyson edited a Black Paper entitled *Fight for Education* in which they proposed tests for all at seven, eleven and fourteen. British industry added its voice, with the managing director of GEC entitling an article 'I Blame the Teachers', in which he held them responsible for the shortcomings of the manufacturing industry.

The Prime Minister, James Callaghan, weighed in with a speech at Ruskin College in October 1976. Simon again gives a useful summary, recounting what Callaghan said as follows:

'I take it that no one claims exclusive rights in this field. Public interest is strong and legitimate and will be satisfied. We spend six billion a year on education, so there will be discussion.' ... he was concerned at complaints from industry that new recruits sometimes do not have the basic tools to do the job that is required; and also that industry is shunned by the fully educated, and that there appears to be a lack of relation between schools and industry...

There is, he suggested, a good case for 'a basic curriculum' with 'universal standards'. As far as educational aims are concerned there has been imbalance. Children should be fitted both for a lively constructive place in society and to do a job of work. The former has been stressed at the expense of the latter... The main issue was to achieve higher standards all round due to the complexity of the world we live in. (Simon, *Education and the Social Order*)

That started it. In 1988, when Margaret Thatcher was Prime Minister, Kenneth Baker, Secretary of State for Education, introduced sweeping reforms with the Education Reform Act, including the National Curriculum and its assessment, schools' responsibility for their finances, and a market for school admissions supported by league tables of school results. In 1992 an Education Act established the Office for Standards in Education (Ofsted). Each successive year saw new legislation and school regulation.

Famously, in 1997, when he became Prime Minister, Tony Blair said his policy would be 'education, education, education': his New Labour administration, and subsequently Gordon Brown's, increased substantially the funding of schools, but continued the practice of regularly introducing new legislation promoting new types of school, weakening the local authorities' role in education, slowly replacing public service with private business, and expecting market forces to enhance the quality of schools.

Then came the Conservative/Lib-Dem coalition, with Michael Gove as Secretary of State for the now-termed Department of Education slashing the previous administrations' Building Schools for the Future plans, abolishing several school quangoes and the General Teaching Council, actively encouraging parents to set up 'free' schools, giving academy status to 'outstanding' schools rather than, as before, to struggling schools, ordering the National Curriculum to be rewritten ... and much else – in a great rush.

Since 1988 there have been twelve Secretaries of State.[1] As Barry Shearman, the long-serving chair of the House of Commons Select Committee on Education (until 2010), said: 'A school that was changing its leadership as regularly would be put in special measures immediately.' For a fascinating account of this period (and earlier), see Derek Gillard's *Education in England: A Brief History* (2007).[2]

Why goodbye?

So, why do I argue that we should say 'goodbye' to Ofsted, Sats and league tables?

Regrettably – nay, catastrophically – they inhibit the freedom of collegial schools to develop their own curriculum and pattern of schooling and, through self-evaluation, to ensure that it is good. If every school is a good school and every child attends first the local primary school and then the local secondary school, parents no longer suffer the agony of choosing, and so league tables are irrelevant and unnecessary. In terms of accountability, a much better system is available arising from the concept of collegial schools, as described in Chapter 7.

Likewise, we should bid farewell to the wide variety of schools which in recent years have come into being. The local school must take in everyone, irrespective of aptitude, ability, faith or parental aspiration, and because of that, everyone working in the school must strive to ensure that it is a good school. Irrespective of differences, the children of a school need to

---

[1] As of January 2011.
[2] http://www.educationengland.org.uk/history

learn to accept each other and work together in the common interest of all. They are the seed bed for the growth of vibrant local communities.

Because the National Curriculum, Sat testing, Ofsted inspections and performance tables are dominant features of government control of schooling, it is incumbent on me to give a detailed explanation of why they should go.

Goodbye National Curriculum[1]

The National Curriculum deskills teachers, restricting their creativity and narrowing the experience of children. Teachers in collegial schools, not government, should make curricular decisions.

Disastrous impact of the changing National Curriculum

Anyone who has watched the changes in the National Curriculum since its inception in the Education Reform Act of 1988 must despair to have seen one generation of children drilled one way and the next another. Ring-binder after ring-binder was sent to schools, full of circulars telling teachers what to teach as determined by small groups of so-called experts.

One of the worst features of the National Curriculum is that it is subject-based, and although designed by well-meaning people, it is blinkered by their concerns for their subject. Each of the government-appointed National Curriculum subject committees has doggedly focused on the perceived vital importance of its own subject – to the exclusion of the rest.

---

[1] These 'goodbye' sections are based on my website, at: http://www.free-school-from-government-control.com

Mathematicians, historians, geographers, scientists, artists, musicians all have a multitude of ideas as to what should go into the National Curriculum. But they forget the old challenge to teachers: do you teach your subject, or do you teach children?

Perhaps the clearest example of the danger of making national decisions as to what every child should do at school lies in the field of literature. Committees and then ministers have decided what books should be studied. David Blunkett (1997–2001) insisted on George Orwell's *Animal Farm* and Aldous Huxley's *Brave New World* being in the lists for 11–14-year-olds to read; Alan Johnson (2006–2007) took them out. Michael Gove, Secretary for Education (2010–), has said:

> The great tradition of our literature – Dryden, Pope, Swift, Byron, Keats, Shelley, Austen, Dickens and Hardy – should be at the heart of school life.

He is also on record as advocating

> [a] traditional education, sitting in rows, learning the kings and queens of England, the great works of literature, proper mental arithmetic, algebra by the age of 11, modern foreign languages. That's the best training of the mind and that's how children will be able to compete.

To anyone outside the hothouse of the Westminster village it is obvious that it should be teachers who decide, in the light of their knowledge of their pupils and their own reading, what literature should be taught in their classes.

Throughout the second half of the twentieth century, while subject-based teaching traditionally dominated secondary schools, this was not considered necessarily the best way to structure a primary school curriculum. But when Kenneth Baker (Secretary of State) introduced the structure for the National Curriculum in 1988 it was designed on the assumption that each subject would develop from Year 1 – that is, five-year-olds. It was argued that this would facilitate the progression of learning as pupils moved from one school to another, particularly the transfer at age 11 from primary to secondary school. It represents a complete failure to understand the differences between primary and secondary schools.

In primary schools this damaged the common practice of concentrating on themes or topics which embraced a variety of disciplines. It led to rigid timetabling and a very fragmented experience of education for young children. Fewer secondary schools worked around themes, but there were some successful experiments in getting away from a 35-period subject-based week – which withered when the National Curriculum arrived.

It is probably true that for weaker teachers and their classes the National Curriculum was a godsend because it put a coherent structure into their work and told them what to do. For able teachers used to making their own decisions, it was devastating, however: it began to deskill them.

Curriculum should be decided by collegial schools, not government

Of course children need to learn to read, write and do simple calculations. Throughout the twentieth century, and long before the National Curriculum came into being, these were taught as essentials and no one said otherwise.

But beyond these essential elements in a curriculum is an enormous range of worthwhile activities that are all educational but do not have the need to be compulsory and be applied uniformly throughout the country. Their inclusion in the curriculum should depend on what talents the school can offer.

Yes, it is great that children learn to swim, make music, sing, dance, paint, and draw. Certainly some sense of historical events and geographical concepts is valuable – but it is absurd for central government to try to determine what events and places should be studied. Enquiry into the physical, natural and mathematical world is important. Environmental exploration and community work are worthwhile. Youth hostel visits and camping events not only stimulate interest in the out-of-doors world, they are also important social experiences for children who may have never left home without their parents. Spiritual growth matters for many parents. But none of these should be laid down by a London-based government and its specialist agencies. Their inclusion or otherwise should be left to schools to decide, in relation to their knowledge of the children in the school, maybe in discussion with parents, but certainly in the light of the knowledge, skills, values and enthusiasm of the teaching staff. It is what a collegial school should do and what teachers should learn to do in their training.

What would happen if the National Curriculum became non-obligatory?

No doubt for a time many schools would continue as before. Slowly staff would gain confidence in themselves to make curriculum decisions based on their own talents and interests, while bearing in mind the needs of children to experience as rounded and balanced an education as possible. The guidance booklets of the National Curriculum could sit on the staffroom shelves to act as a resource when needed. They contain a wealth of ideas that are valuable when choice is the guiding principle, but not when uptake of subjects is compulsory.

With choice, teachers' creative energy would flow and their enthusiasm for teaching flourish. Young people of all ages would be much more likely than they are now to enjoy school thoroughly, learn effectively, develop their individual talents, and gain a love of learning which will illumine their whole lives. Teachers would 'walk tall' in our society and establish their proper role as guardians of the future.

Goodbye SATS

Sats testing was valuable originally...

When Professor Paul Black (of King's College London) and his Task Group on Assessment and Testing (TGAT, set up by Kenneth Baker, Secretary of State for Education and Science) developed the idea of Sats originally in 1987, they called them Standard Assessment Tasks. Seven-year-olds – and their teachers – first engaged with these tasks in 1991. They were initially fun for the children, if arduous and time-consuming for the teachers, but the enormous achievement was that, over the next few years, every primary school teacher in the country learned the value of effective assessment and how it facilitates the progression of learning. Some teachers had always known this, but the result of it being introduced nationally by the Education Reform Act of 1988 meant that every teacher became trained in assessment: it was the greatest achievement of that Act.

TGAT introduced the concept of levels of achievement, ranging from 1 to 10, which pupils would move through from age 5 to age 16, with national assessments being made at ages 7, 11, 14 and 16. This scale was defined as a straight line progression from Level 2 for the average seven-year-old in each subject, to the boundary between Levels 6 and 7 for the average 16-year-old. TGAT recognised that there were difficulties in relating this to GSCE grades, and shortly the testing was restricted to ages 7, 11 and 14 and the scale was only normally used in terms of Levels 1 to 8. (The situation as of November 2010 was that these assessments were made by pupils' own teachers, using government-supplied materials, at age seven (English and mathematics) and age 14 (English, mathematics, science and other foundation subjects); with externally marked assessments at age 11 – in English and mathematics.)

... but then government moved the goal posts

Governments, both Conservative and Labour, steadily changed the TGAT system. Whereas TGAT had said 'the average expectation for an age 11 pupil will be Level 4' (in paragraph 108), the word 'average' was quietly dropped by government, and Level 4 became the expectation for all pupils. Sats were renamed Standard Attainment Tests and more recently changed again to National Curriculum Tests (though nobody outside the Department seems to use the term!). TGAT recommended strongly that the results of national assessment for an individual school should '*only*' (one of the few words underlined in the report) be published 'as part of a broader report by that school of its work as a whole' because there are 'many factors outside its control that affect its work'. Government rejected this and tables of results were published, with numbers naked of any context.

TGAT recognised that Sats would involve more work for teachers, but never envisaged that it would also stress children and their parents. Now, year by year, it is reported that schools are increasingly teaching to the test in order to score high and avoid harassment from Ofsted inspections, and it is this that is causing children and their parents to suffer from stress. The 2008 report by the House of Commons Select Committee for Children, Schools and Families said:

Many witnesses argued that testing is stressful for children. Moreover, repeated testing has a negative effect on children, leading to demotivation, reduced learning potential and lower educational outcomes... Witnesses have expressed concern that the levels of accountability in schools are resulting in the disillusionment of children.

Children not reaching the target standard at a given stage have the impression that they have 'failed' whilst they may, in fact, have made perfectly acceptable progress... Teaching to the test and narrowing of the curriculum are also thought to have a negative effect on children.

The resulting lack of creativity in teaching impacts on children's enjoyment of a subject and their motivation to learn. (Paras 150–153)

Seven arguments in favour of Sats assessment and reasons for refuting them

1. **'Sats assessments support classroom learning.'** The essential reason for assessing a pupil is to see what educational progress is being made, and hence determine what the pupil should do next. It enables the teacher to ensure regularly that work is geared to steady progress. It is self-evident that a set of tests at the end of primary education is of no use in assessment for learning. The statement from the government website for parents that 'Your child will take national tests at the end of Key Stage 2... This helps the school to make plans for their future learning' overlooks the fact that the children leave the school shortly after taking the tests! ***Verdict: Sats cannot support classroom learning.***

2. **'Sats results inform parents of their child's progress.'**
   Does it really help parents to be told, when the child
   leaves primary school, 'Your child is at Level 4 in English,
   maths and science'? What are needed are regular written
   reports on the child's progress across the curriculum
   and the opportunity to discuss progress with the class
   teacher; as a result of successful government initiatives
   this is now standard practice in primary schools across
   the country. Relationships between teachers and parents
   support the ongoing education of the children – bland
   Sats numbers do not helpfully inform parents. *Verdict:*
   Sats give inadequate information, and too late, to parents.

3. **'Sats results help parents choose their child's school.'**
   Rural and many suburban areas rarely offer a choice of
   primary schools within easy distance of home. In urban
   areas there may be a choice of several primary schools,
   and the best way of choosing is to visit each school,
   read the prospectus and the recent self-evaluation report
   and, above all, talk to other parents. SAT results for 11-
   year-olds are of little help since much can change in the
   six years before the incoming child leaves. League tables
   in local newspapers do not help parents choose a school.
   They make for good gossip but poor guidance! *Verdict:*
   Sats do not help parental choice in a meaningful way.

4. **'Sats results provide accountability of schools.'** Since
   schools are funded from the public purse they should
   be accountable to the public. Nobody challenges that.
   But Sats results are a poor indicator of whether there
   is 'value for money'. Schools are not on a level playing
   field: however good the teaching is, the social
   environment has a large effect on children's achievements.

Public accountability should be through a school's governing body. This body, democratically chosen to represent parents and other sections of the community, and supported by the local authority, should recognise the achievements and potential of the school, comprehend the problems of the catchment area, and judge the school accordingly. Local knowledge is best for tackling local issues. Governors should challenge and support the work of a school while trusting the professionalism of teachers in terms of their integrity and determination to do what is best for each pupil. Such an approach will put to good use the substantial investment that has been made by government into training school governors. *Verdict: Sats provide a poor form of accountability.*

5. **'Sats results provide national monitoring of standards.'**
   It seems to be a national pastime to speculate whether educational standards are rising or falling. Politicians use the Sats results either to praise the achievements of their own party or to lambast their opponents. But academics find, on the basis of research, that the evidence is too problematic for such speculation to be meaningful. Year by year like is not being compared with like. As the Select Committee noted:

   > the purpose of national monitoring of the education system, particularly for policy formation, is best served by sample testing to measure standards over time and ... cohort testing is neither appropriate nor, in our view, desirable for this purpose. We recommend further that, in the interests of public confidence, such sample testing should be carried

out by a body at arms-length from the Government. (Para 186)

Rigorous sample monitoring across the country would be much more effective, as was the case before a Conservative administration abolished the Assessment of Performance Unit. *Verdict: Sats are not a valid tool for measuring changes in national educational standards.*

6. **'Sats assessments give continuity in education when pupils transfer from primary to secondary school.'** Originally this was seen as an important use of Key Stage 2 Sats results. But many secondary schools now choose to test the children on arrival rather than use Sats data from the primary feeder schools. As the *Independent* reported on 18 July 2008: 'Most secondary schools have already introduced their own tests because they do not believe the Sats are a reliable indicator of the pupils' ability.' *Verdict: Sats are no longer an aid to transfer between schools.*

7. **'Sats assessment is a tool for raising standards in schools in order to sustain future economic growth.'** We are constantly being told by the world of business that the national workforce has insufficient people with the skills that will be needed in the future for our economy to remain competitive in world markets. This seems to be a major reason for putting pressure on schools to ensure that greater numbers of pupils achieve the 'expected' levels in the Sats and later at GCSE, etc. But claims that standards are rising due to this pressure are being challenged on the grounds that schools are increasingly 'teaching to the test', to the

detriment of an all-round education. As the Select Committee said:

> We received substantial evidence that teaching to the test, to an extent which narrows the curriculum and puts sustained learning at risk, is widespread... We have no doubt that teachers generally have the very best intentions in terms of providing the best education they can for their pupils. However, the way that many teachers have responded to the Government's approach to accountability has meant that test results are pursued at the expense of a rounded education for children. (Para 130)

So, it is highly doubtful whether the future economic health of the nation is being aided by primary school Sats, while the needs of employers for creative workers who can collaborate and work in teams are being side-tracked. Beyond this, it is also uncertain, with global warming and unpredictable climate change, whether competitive struggle for dominance in world markets will be a prime national concern when our young people reach adulthood. What is certain is that while young people obviously need a good command of mathematics and English, they also need a broad and balanced education which develops their talents in many dimensions so that individually and collectively they can respond to the mounting problems of a troubled world. *Verdict: It is doubtful whether Sats are helpful to the future economic health of the country.*

If Sats go, how will it affect schools?

It will mean that children will not be externally tested at the end of KS2. Teachers will make their own assessments, using test materials if they deem it necessary, so that they can communicate to parents and to secondary schools the levels of attainment of individual pupils at the time of leaving the primary school.

In getting rid of Sats it must also be firmly established that teachers' assessments will not be collected, collated and put into league tables by government or anybody else. Nor should anybody outside schools try to make value-added assessments. As a result, the government will save money by no longer preparing, printing, distributing, collecting and marking test papers, collating results and publishing these results.

As a result of these changes primary schools will not need to prepare children for external testing in English and mathematics – but they can engage with the normal processes of teaching these subjects and the rest of the curriculum in an atmosphere untrammelled by preparation for testing.

The levels of attainment in English and mathematics, as originally devised by Professor Black and his task group, should be retained. They have become an invaluable part of the assessment process which is now recognised by all teachers as essential to good teaching. Class teachers in primary schools, spending most of their time with one class, should have a clear idea of the level of attainment of each child. This should be communicated to parents perhaps once a year – but not to any agency outside the school. It is helpful for teachers to have available simple test instruments so that they can check on their judgements, but this should not be made into a big deal.

Will standards in English and mathematics drop or climb if Sats go?

Schools should collate the results of teachers' assessments at the end of each of the two key stages, and reflect on and evaluate any changes from year to year – but because of the natural variation to be expected in these figures between one year-group of children and the next, they should not be published outside the school, or collected by government agencies.

What is certain is that there will be improvement in the standard of all-round education because teachers and pupils will be no longer constrained by the testing regime and so more time will be available for all parts of the curriculum.

Of course, government should know what is happening to the standards of education across the country, but instead of the phoney use of KS2 statistics, the careful testing of a randomly selected sample group of schools around the country, year by year, will indicate whether standards are moving. This should be part of the function of the National Education Council described in Chapter 7.

The procedure for transfer to secondary education in the absence of Sats

Secondary schools expect that new entrants will have good skills of literacy and numeracy. A reasonable assumption is that Level 4, as assessed by primary school teachers, is an appropriate definition of the standards of literacy and numeracy that are needed for pupils to tackle successfully the curriculum of secondary schools. To achieve this for all pupils should be a proper aim for a primary school – and written into its prospectus as issued to parents.

However, almost inevitably, there will be some children who, at the end of Year 6, at age 11, have not yet achieved Level 4.

For all sorts of reasons they may not be progressing at the same rate as some of their fellows. It is well known by teachers and most parents that children develop at different rates, and to 'expect' everyone to have reached a particular level at a particular time is contrary to the substantial evidence of child development.

So, if they need the competence of Level 4 for their secondary school studies, they need:

- either to stay another year in primary education
- or to work in a special group when they transfer to secondary school.

The former is probably the better route. What is important is that the school tries hard to avoid any social stigma and strives to overcome the difficulties for individuals who see their mates moving on while they have to stay behind. It is an inevitable consequence of the fact that we learn at different rates – the tortoise gets there but needs longer. If the school is organised with a measure of vertical grouping, so that more than one age group is in the same class, then it is clear to all that some will move on to secondary school and others will stay for another year.

What is certain is that the current oppressive Sats assessment regime enforced by government doesn't prevent about 20% of Year 6 children going to secondary school without having quite reached the 'expected' standard. Putting more pressure on schools, castigating teachers, and threatening heads with the sack are not helpful measures. A better way of ensuring that everybody starts secondary education adequately skilled is needed, as suggested here.

Goodbye Ofsted

School inspection: 1839–2009 – full circle!

In 1839 school inspections by Her Majesty's Inspectors (HMIs) began for elementary schools, and their judgements determined the level of government grant received by these schools. They were feared by teachers in the nineteenth century, but later their role changed to a more benign one of reporting essentially to government on the national state of education. Up to 1992 school inspections were carried out on a limited basis by these HMIs and more generally by local education authority (LEA) inspectors. The practice of the latter was of variable quality: at its best was the 'challenge and support' work where criticisms of a school were linked to advice and support. Central government had no control over the LEA inspectors.

In 1992, in order to ensure that the provisions of the Education Reform Act of 1988 and subsequent government initiatives were fully implemented, the Office for Standards in Education (Ofsted) was established. All schools were to be inspected every few years. Since then it has steadily taken on more and more inspectorial roles and engaged in quasi-research activities.

It is not easy to describe how Ofsted operates, because it constantly changes the ways in which its inspections are conducted. What is certain is that all state schools in England are inspected regularly – the time interval being no longer than six years and in most cases less. Also, the extent of notice has varied from several months to a few days, and the intensity of the visitation has varied from a week in which, in primary schools visited, each teacher was observed at least once for a full lesson, to one-day visits in which the focus was on the head teacher and the school's Sats results. Ofsted carries out its inspections through independently contracted school inspectors, who work strictly to a detailed Framework for Inspection and are trained centrally to do this.

Chris Woodhead, who was chief inspector from 1994 to 2000, told the press that there were 15,000 failing teachers in our schools. This was a gross mis-statement. Ofsted inspectors had given 2 per cent of observed *lessons* in primary schools the lowest grade, and he had extrapolated this to *teachers*, mischievously ignoring the point that one poor lesson doesn't mean that other lessons by that teacher are poor, and for some teachers the presence of an inspector could be terrifying and ruin a lesson.

In Victorian classrooms, fear enforced learning, but this idea was long ago recognised as inhumane and ineffective; it passed out of currency – until Woodhead, by his own admission, re-introduced it as a mechanism for improving the work of teachers. He's gone but the legacy remains. Ofsted inspectors are feared by most teachers. What a way to try to improve education!

The purpose of HMI visits throughout most of the twentieth century was to provide carefully formed judgements on the work of schools and to advise government on the national picture. In the process HMIs produced occasional reports which were helpful to schools and gave invaluable evidence to the major enquiries into education conducted by the Central Advisory Council on Education, such as those known as the Crowther, Newsom and Plowden Reports. HMIs were known for their high intelligence, balanced judgements and exquisite manners. By contrast, Ofsted inspectors often have seemed rule-bound, alien and brash.

Ruthless, narrow-visioned, fear-inducing, undermining, unsupportive

The following objections to Ofsted indicate that it acts as a ruthless enforcer of government policies, with a narrow vision of education which fails to take account of local circumstances; that it is fear-inducing in a way alien to most practitioners of teaching; that it undermines the professional status of teachers; and that it fails to provide support to those needing help.

(1) The first objection arises from the official statement of Ofsted's objective for school inspections as stated in its Strategic Plan for 2006/7:

> To help learners to achieve their full potential by reporting clearly, independently and unambiguously on quality and standards in education.

Ofsted expects schools to achieve standards in education set by national government, and castigates those that don't. But government sets arbitrary standards for all schools, irrespective of local conditions, based on vague presumptions about the future economic needs of the country. For example, in 2009 these were the official standards: in primary schools at least 65% of pupils at Key Stage 2 should achieve Level 4 or higher in English and mathematics, and in secondary schools more than 30% of pupils should gain 5 GCSEs levels A*-C, including English and mathematics.

(2) The second objection arises from the first. Ofsted inspectors are in day-to-day contact with schools and must be acutely aware of the major concerns about government educational policy voiced by professionals on the amount of testing, the constraints imposed by the National Curriculum, and the extent of ministerial interference in the work of schools. But instead of expressing these concerns to ministers and challenging them to realise how counter-productive many of their policies are, Ofsted has chosen consistently to enforce government requirements and ride rough-shod over schools' protestations.

(3) Ofsted sees any shortcomings in a school's work as the fault of the teachers and a failure of management. It discounts the idea that socio-economic factors in the school's environment might contribute to performance problems.

(4) Ofsted inspections are feared by teachers who, perceiving the inspectors as the enemy, may perform abnormally (i.e. better or worse than usual) in the classroom when observed.

(5) Ofsted inspections are feared by head teachers who know that their job can be at stake if the school gets an adverse report.

(6) Ofsted inspection reports challenge schools that are perceived as underachieving, but they offer little assistance in helping the school or individual teachers to improve. Since 2003 Ofsted has adopted a 'naming and shaming policy' which publicly identifies schools put into special measures.

(7) Introduced in 2005, Ofsted letters to pupils after an inspection can undermine the professional relationship between teachers and pupils and between teachers and parents.

(8) Introduced in 2007, Ofsted's email system for parents to complain about schools encourages a culture of complaint.

Ofsted should be abolished – professionals do not need an enforcement agency

The Office for Standards in Education (Ofsted) could have been valuable if it had treated teachers respectfully, as fellow professionals to be inspected cordially, challenged where necessary, and guided and supported when appropriate. But instead it chose to engender fear in those inspected, and, where it found fault, convey its criticisms to public, parents and children in a way that could only undermine confidence in the school and its head.

Instead of challenging the government's model of teachers as technicians, the Ofsted inspectors have acted as factory inspectors ensuring that the workforce obeys the minutiae of the rule book. It acts as an enforcement agency. It is a leviathan, with a culture so alien to the needs of schools that it needs to be swept right away. The culture of engendering fear and disrespectfulness, and of undermining professional confidence is so ingrained in the Ofsted system that tinkering with it is pointless. It should be abolished, with a massive saving in public expenditure.

Without the threat of Ofsted, head teachers would be free to treat the constant flow of government initiatives as either useful guidelines to act on in their own judgement, or as fodder for the recycling bin. At present any deviation from government diktats is a potential threat to a head's job.

Without Ofsted, how will standards rise?

The answer lies in the self-monitoring of collegial schools. Teachers no longer work in isolation from each other. The days of the closed classroom are long gone. Teachers cooperate, share problems and learn from one another. Primary school heads wander in and out of classrooms, know the strengths and weaknesses of their teachers, and can try to help where necessary. Likewise, school governors visit classrooms, and though they may lack professional insight, they can ask common-sense questions and offer man-in-the-street comments on what they observe. And as a back-up, heads and governors can obtain the willing help of other schools, as well as of local authority inspectors working to the rubric of 'challenge and support'.

Professor John MacBeath, of Cambridge University, has pioneered ways of self-evaluation – with five books on the subject. His message is that self-evaluation is an essential part of a teacher's day-to-day work and that schools should be always asking themselves what they should be doing next in the best interests of their pupils.

Ofsted has tried to develop the idea of self-evaluation, with a manual for schools to use full of tick boxes, followed up by Ofsted inspections to check whether schools have ticked the right boxes. But self-evaluation is not like that. As MacBeath says, 'Self-evaluation is a process of discovery rather than a tedious adherence to a well-trodden trail.'

The saturation point for raising standards has been reached in primary schools.

Figure 1 shows the combined national results for 11-year-olds tested in English, mathematics and science for the years 1997 to 2009 at the end of Key Stage Two (KS2) (there are no comparable data for 2010 because the science tests were dropped in that year). If every 11-year-old child in England had reached Level 4 in each subject, the height of the bars would be 300. That is what the government 'expects'. In practice, notwithstanding enormous pressure put on primary schools,

Figure 1
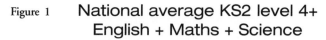

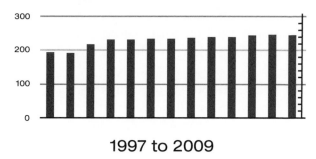

1997 to 2009

the nation's children are levelling out at just below the 250 mark.

It is recognised by teachers (and most parents), but not by politicians, that children develop at different rates, and it may well be that an average score of between 200 and 250 represents the optimum score for the population of our children aged around 11. Give them, say, another year of good primary schooling, or careful support in the first year of secondary school, and they will nearly all reach the 300 mark – that is, achieve Level 4+ in all three subjects by around age 12.

As noted above, it needs to be remembered that when in 1987 TGAT developed the system of levels, Level 4 was to be the *average* for 11-year-olds, not the *expectation* for all.

Figure 2 shows similar test data for 7-year-olds at the end of Key Stage One (KS1). Until 2004 these tests were administered externally, but since then they have been administered by schools without time limits and as part of ongoing classroom activity. The government has provided schools with the tests to be used and has continued to collect the results, but publishes these only at local authority and national level; unlike KS2, the results are not published for individual schools at this level.

Figure 2

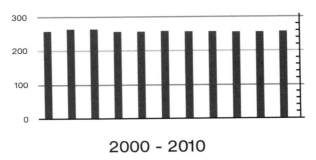

National average KS1 level 2+
Reading + Writing + Maths

2000 - 2010

99

Figure 2 combines results for reading, writing and maths. If every 7-year-old child in England had reached Level 2 in each of these the height of the bars would be 300. That is what the government 'expects'. Clearly, as with KS2, notwithstanding constant pressure from the government, the national performance at this age has levelled out. Again, it should be remembered that TGAT had defined Level 2 as the average performance at this age, not as the expectation for all.

It seems clear from the charts shown in these two figures that primary schools have reached the optimum level that can be achieved. They provide clear evidence that children develop at different rates and that some just are not ready at age 7 or age 11 to meet the expectations of Level 2 and Level 4. The pressure from government and its enforcement agency Ofsted has achieved little in the last ten years. It is time to take their relentless pressure off – indeed, that should have been done several years ago.

Goodbye league tables

Performance tables showing the assessment results of schools were introduced in 1992 when John Patten was Secretary of State and John Major Prime Minister. They were pounced on by the newspapers, who turned them into league tables, praising those at the top and pillorying those at the bottom. Mainly they consisted of Sats results for primary schools and GCSE and A-level results for secondary schools, but over the years they became more complicated as value-added measures, truancy levels and other statistics were also reported. Michael Gove says he is going to report on levels of teacher sickness soon!

The government claimed that making these data public would

help parents to choose schools and encourage those near the bottom of lists to improve. The teacher unions, however, were all opposed to them. This statement by the NASUWT expresses the concerns of the teaching profession vigorously and unambiguously. It says that the annual league tables

> encourage competition, discourage full collaboration, place schools under unacceptable pressure, cause teachers to teach to the tests and undermine their confidence in their own professional judgement. The tables feed a culture of focusing on the alleged failures of the system rather than the significant achievements of pupils and teachers: achievements which are secured despite the league tables, not because of them. The high-stakes performance league tables, with the serious consequences for schools of perceived failure, make them at best cautious about using professional flexibility and at worst resistant, distorting and narrowing decisions about curriculum content and pedagogy. They are neither relevant nor effective and should be abolished.

Agreed. Also, in the scenario of this book, in which every school is, and is perceived as, a good school, serving the local community, there will be no purpose in the enormous effort which the civil service put into collecting, collating and publishing school data. (Nor will there be Sats results.) Instead, it is hoped that local newspapers will publish reports from their local schools; these should prove to be much more informative and interesting to their readers.

Sadly it is going to take time before government is prepared to reject league tables. *The Times Educational Supplement* reported in March 2011 that Michael Gove, Secretary of State, had announced that 'super-league tables' are planned for 2012. He said:

We will publish as much data as possible so parents and teachers can really see what is going on in schools. This proper transparency will drive best practice and accountability across all schools.

Would that Mr Gove would take heed of the following section!

'It is vain to do with more what can be done with less'

The above was said by William of Ockham (or Occam) in the fourteenth century. When it is taxpayers' money that is being used to do with more what could be done with less it is not vain, it is politically foolhardy and financially scandalous. But when it is children's education that is bedevilled by more, in the form of excessive testing, obsessive inspection and a restrictive curriculum, it is morally wrong and totally unacceptable.

Political action is needed to take Occam's razor to Sats formal testing, league tables of school results, Ofsted inspections, the National Curriculum and government micro-management, and excise them from the English system of national education.

This book is mainly about the kind of education that young people should have had by the time they are adults and the 'inevitable' happens – the time when our economic system, essentially based on continuous growth, turbo-consumerism, massive inequality between the greedy rich and the needy poor, and a competitive me-first culture, collapses. I realise that at present only a few of us recognise that this is, as I argue, inevitable. So I also realise that some of the ideas of Chapters 8 onwards may not be recognised yet as viable approaches to the education that will be needed. The general public, and, indeed, many in the teaching profession, have as yet to comprehend the urgent need for these approaches – which is, of course, the rationale for this book. But the call to wield Occam's razor and excise deleterious and unnecessary features of today's educational system in England, coupled with the suggestions on effective accountability in the next chapter, could be implemented immediately. They would, I believe, be welcomed both by the teaching profession and by most parents of young children.

If ...

If the great departments of state, like the Home Office, the Foreign Office or Treasury, were closed down, the nation would fall apart. But, strangely, if the Department of Education were to disappear, provided the Treasury continued to provide funding for schools, apart from a large number of people becoming unemployed, there would be no difference to the education of the young. Children would continue to go to school. Teachers would continue to teach to the best of their ability. Parents would continue to value the schools their children attended. So...?

7

Effective Accountability: Bottom-up, Not Top-down

What is accountability? 'An iceberg: menacing'?

Wikipedia struggles with the term:

> Accountability is a concept with several meanings. It is often used synonymously with such concepts as responsibility, answerability, blameworthiness, liability, and other terms associated with the expectation of account-giving... As a term related to governance, accountability has been difficult to define.

Accountability seems to be part of the managerialism that has swept through western society, along with devices such as targets, league tables, bench-marks, inspection, and blaming-and-shaming. It is part of a managerial culture that seems to expect workers to be lazy and incompetent unless their work is thoroughly monitored and supervised by a hierarchy that, in turn, is held accountable by an even higher body. Starting in the business world of industry and commerce, it has been pushed into the professions.

A report by the Royal College of Nursing, *Interpreting Accountability* (by Savage and Moore, 2004) refers to considerable ambiguity attached to the concept of accountability that reflected the 'catch all' use of the term in current government policy. The term was often taken to mean responsibility, partly in the sense of deserving blame or credit... It seemed beyond precise definition. It was like an iceberg: menacing, only partially knowable, and its full shape could only be assumed.

In my understanding, professionals are people who, having studied hard and served an apprenticeship, carry out services for clients to the best of their ability, following the standards of their profession, and in ways which are deemed by them to be in the best interests of clients, who may not be able to judge that this is the case; in return, they are paid for their services. The professions have plenary bodies which define their standards and can penalise or expel members who step outside the ethical standards expected of them. The Law Society, the General Medical Council and the various chartered bodies have their disciplinary procedures. Education has been less successful in establishing a united professional body for oversight of its practitioners; the General Teaching Council, set up by a Labour government and about to be abolished by the present coalition government, struggled to establish this role.

Today, 'accountability' is demanded of professionals by governments that do not seem to have a clear idea of what they are asking for – or what the consequences of that may be. Since large amounts of public money are spent on, for example, teachers, doctors and nurses, it can be seen as right that government, on behalf of taxpayers, should want to see that it is being spent well, even if, as argued above, that is built into their professional ethic. But government, having probed professional work with the rolled umbrella of accountability to ensure financial probity, then unfurls it to try and meet government-set targets of achievement, health and safety standards, equal opportunity norms, anti-racism measures, and training goals. As the Royal College of Nursing report said, accountability is 'only partially knowable, and its full shape can only be assumed'.

Trust – the traditional alternative to accountability

If managers trust the workers to pull their weight, if patients trust the doctors and nurses to tackle their ailments to the best of their ability, if parents trust the teachers to educate their children effectively, there is no need for accountability.

On the odd occasion when a worker, doctor, nurse or teacher breaks that trust, there should be, and there are, disciplinary and legal mechanisms for dealing with the situation. The creation of vast systems of bureaucracy, checking and counter-checking on what is happening, is unnecessary and counterproductive. Not only could the time and effort that goes into this be used more productively, but the very existence of checking systems gives an expectation that people will try to cheat unless they are under surveillance.

Sadly, but significantly, the rise of demands for accountability is associated with an erosion of trust in people. A few years back Libby Purves wrote in *The Times* (20 May 2003):

> Comparative surveys over 40 years suggest that British trustfulness has halved: in the 1950s 60 per cent of us answered 'Yes, most people can be trusted', in the 1980s 44 per cent, today only 29 per cent.

Such data depend on exactly how the question asked is framed and the answers collated. There can be little doubt about the trend downhill, even if an ICM poll of January 2010 is much more sanguine. It asked: 'Do you agree or disagree that most people can be trusted?' Giving the responses in terms of those who 'tend to agree', it reported that 64 per cent did. Probably the difference between 29% saying 'Yes, most people can be trusted' and, at around the same time (but in a different survey), 64% 'tending to agree that most people can be trusted' is the difference between 'I agree' and 'I tend to agree'.

It is the detail of the ICM survey that tells a worrying story. Age analysis shows these percentages 'tending to agree that most people can be trusted': 18–24-year-olds – 38%; 25–54-year-olds – 48%; 55–64-year-olds – 67%, 64-year-olds and older – 71%; overall – 64%. Will the young become less lacking in trust as they become older – or will they retain their cynicism?

What becomes more interesting is to know which groups of people are highly trusted, and which not. Over the last 27 years Ipsos MORI has been conducting in-home, face-to-face interviews regularly with samples of about 2,000 people. One question is worded as follows:

Now I will read out a list of different types of people. For each, would you tell me whether you generally trust them to tell the truth or not?

The list includes doctors, teachers, business leaders, journalists, and government ministers. Table 4 shows the percentages, over the years, of respondents saying *these people tell the truth.*

On this evidence I would suggest that accountability is needed for business leaders, journalists and government ministers, but less so for doctors and teachers!

Nevertheless, accountability is so embedded in our present-day culture that it would be foolish to suggest that there should be none in education. What I will assert, however, as in an

Table 4. 'Who tells the truth?' (Ipsos MORI polls 1983–2009)

	1983	1993	2000	2003	2006	2009
Doctors	82	84	87	91	92	92
Teachers	79	84	85	87	88	88
TV news readers	63	72	73	66	66	63
Business leaders	25	32	28	28	31	25
Journalists	19	10	15	18	19	22
Government ministers	16	11	21	20	22	16

earlier chapter, is that Ofsted reports and league tables of school results are very poor instruments of accountability. They should be abolished and a different concept and system of accountability introduced.

The present system of accountability

At present, the accountability system for schools in England is roughly trying to ensure:

- that parents should know which schools are judged 'good' so that they can choose them for their offspring;
- that parents should know how their children are progressing;
- that local government and national government should know whether individual schools are spending their funds wisely and with probity;
- that local government and national government should know how individual schools are raising their standards of achievement; and
- that the nation should know whether national standards are improving.

The first of these is irrelevant once, as argued in this book, children attend the local school and every school is a 'good' school. The second does not require external agencies, but is a matter of teachers and parents in regular communication with each other. The third is a matter for local auditors appointed by and reporting to the school governors. The fourth is a bigger issue than expressed in this bullet point. It should be concerned with how the school is striving to educate every child in the broadest sense of 'education'. It should be communicated to parents and local community as well as local government – and, in some brief and digestible form, to national government. The fifth point, in the way that it is currently sought, is a hallucination – a perception without stimulus. It is simply not possible to try to say anything meaningful year by year from averaged GCSE or 11-year-old Sats results, or from numbers of A* grades at A level or first-class degree awards. The nearest that one can get to it is to administer the same test procedure to sample groups of young people over several years, as was done by the Assessment of Performance Unit (APU) until Margaret Thatcher, in her 'wisdom', abolished it.

A better approach to accountability

Yes, it is important that schools are accountable. Obviously they should be accountable for the considerable sums of public money that they spend but also, more importantly, for the all-round quality of education they provide for the young. Present-day inspections and league tables are expensive to operate, inadequate in their findings, and seriously distort what should be the proper all-round education of children.

The following outline shows how school accountability could start with parents and move through school governors, local community, local administration, a National Education Council, to Parliament. Some of the procedures are already in place.

➢ **Parents** – leave things as they are now, but enhance opportunities. These measures would ensure the parents are well informed about the education of their children and can contribute to its success:
  - they should receive detailed reports of their child's progress from teachers and meet them regularly;
  - if there are concerns, they should without difficulty be able to arrange meetings with teachers;
  - they should be able to read about the local school's aims and curriculum and how it operates;
  - they should be able to seek to influence the school's aims and curriculum through promoting discourse in the local community and discussions with governors;
  - they should be able to seek election as school governor;
  - they should be able to make visits to the school.

➢ **Teachers and head** – leave things as they are now, but enhance certain practices:
  - they should work collegially under the leadership of the head in striving for the best education;
  - they should make regular assessment of children's work and involve a partnership school to moderate these judgements;
  - they should make detailed reports of each child's progress to parents and meet them regularly;
  - if there are concerns, they should arrange meetings with parents;
  - they should regularly evaluate their own work (using research-based self-evaluation procedures);
  - these evaluation findings should be included in head's reports to school governors.

➢ **School governors** – mainly leave things as they are as

now, but enhance certain practices to ensure that governors play a central role in accountability:

- they should be elected by the local community, perhaps at same time as local councillors;
- they should discuss termly reports from head about educational work and progress of the school;
- they should be expected to visit classrooms, and talk to teachers, parents and others about work of the school;
- they should be prepared to challenge and support the school staff from a lay perspective when they deem it necessary;
- through their finance committee they should have oversight of the school's expenditure and ensure that it is properly audited;
- they should work with the head teacher in the appointment and dismissal of staff;
- they should work with the head teacher to prepare an annual report to the local administration.

➢ **Local community**:
  - should be responsible for electing school governors;
  - should have ready access to an annual report of each local school as printed in local newspapers. (This would be in place of today's ridiculous league tables.) This measure would be likely to generate local interest in the work of the school and create a sense of 'our' local school.

➢ **Local administration** (note use of the term 'admini-strations' rather than 'authorities', as discussed in Chapter 4):
  - should engage in careful discussion with local

communities in order to identify catchment areas for primary and secondary schools;

- should employ local school inspectors (in place of Ofsted inspectors) who give professional 'challenge and support' to schools;
- should collect and draw together school annual reports in order to communicate salient matters annually to a National Education Council.

➤ **National Education Council** (this is the one national 'quango' that I look for in education):

- there should be an independent National Education Council with a balanced membership of teachers' leaders, MPs, academics and other prominent members of society;
- it should be funded by government but independent of it;
- it would arrange nationwide sample monitoring of basic skills;
- it would collate evidence from local administrations' reports;
- it would commission research on key issues that it identifies;
- it would report biannually on the state of education nationwide to Parliament.

➤ **Parliament:**

- every two years it should receive and debate a report from the National Education Council on the state of education nationwide;
- a summary of Parliament's deliberations should be sent to every school for discussion by staff and governors on whether any changes in the school's policies are merited;

113

- this should be the starting point for such future legislation that the education system may need. Parliament would identify any significant issues and urge the government to draw up appropriate legislation.

What I have set out here is a coherent system of accountability which would be 'bottom-up' and not, as at present, 'top-down'. It would create a clear-cut route linking schools to parliamentary debate. It would enable changes in education to arise from evidence, collected slowly, critically and systematically. It would put responsibility for accountability locally into the lap of governing bodies. It would put the agency of change into the debating chambers of Parliament. Hopefully it would take educational policies out of the ideologies and manifestos of the political parties and away from the whims of individual ministers. It would create a truly democratic way of ensuring that every child receives a good education.

8

Creating Conviviality, and Teaching About It

In Chapter 2, I gave a framework definition of education involving the concepts of nurture, culture and survival. The first of these is described there as 'the experience and nurture of personal and social development towards worthwhile living'. In the present chapter I set out an approach to 'worthwhile living' involving an element that I believe to be essential for a viable future: conviviality.

Espousing conviviality as a life-directing ethos has many consequences for those, like teachers, who are contributing to the future of their community, their country and the world. The ethos of conviviality, as the joy that comes from being in harmony with one's environment, one's fellows and oneself, has many facets. It embraces ideas of ecological sustainability, social justice, elimination of poverty at home and worldwide, peace, community, and democracy.

It is important to recognise that the alternative life-directing ethos of wealth creation is essential for a poverty-stricken community or country in order to begin to establish a satisfying quality of life for its members. This means that beyond the basic needs of food, water, shelter and security, people can at least enjoy the happiness of family life and social intercourse with their fellows; gain the education that is an entry to the culture of their time and provides them with the skills needed for their adult life; access good health provision to tackle such ailments as may afflict them; and have opportunities for democratic participation in the affairs of their society.

But once this quality of life has been achieved and a society moves on to reach the boundary between decent need and obscene greed, as is the case for most (but not all) of the populations of the so-called developed countries, the ethos of conviviality is needed, not just because it can be held to be morally right, but because it can save humankind from destroying itself.

While wealth creation has produced prosperity for many people across the world, it has also caused misery for many others. Today it can be seen to be the unfortunate agent of man-made global warming, incipient climate change, essential resource depletion and insidious pollution of air, water and earth. To ameliorate this situation the rich countries of the world need to adopt convivial policies and contract their economies, while the poor countries need to expand theirs to the point where all the economies of the world converge. Hopefully at that stage they will all become convivial.

While wealth creation is the dominant ethos of most businesses and governments, conviviality is often the ethos of families and local communities – by whatever name they call it.

Wealth creation

The prevalent ethos of the macro world of businesses and nations is a way of living where the creation of wealth is seen as an essential activity. Businesses see themselves as successful if their profits rise year by year: their chief executives and senior managers may lose their jobs if this does not happen. Governments are judged by the extent of economic growth during their period in office – in the expectation that growth will not only create work for the unemployed but give greater access to goods and services for all who work hard and hence endlessly strive to improve their quality of life.

Wealth creation puts people in competition with each other, and this is seen as the engine of progress leading to greater affluence. But it is in the nature of competition that there are winners and losers – and usually more of the latter. Wealth creation enables the winners in creating wealth to spend it in order to enhance their own quality of life and enjoy happiness, but it deprives the losers of these opportunities.

Historically, wealth creation has led to remarkable signs of affluence: it has enabled the building of towns, transport systems, communication systems, schools, hospitals, churches; it has funded great architecture, geographic exploration, scientific discovery; it has filled our shops with desirable goods and made many public services widely available.

But wealth creation also has led to devastating levels of misery through the greed and hedonism of those who have put wealth creation for themselves above the needs of others who are less fortunate, skilful, ambitious, or ruthless. Politically, the struggle to create more wealth has pitted nation against nation, sometimes leading to war. Today the ethos of wealth creation is pushing the world towards global socio-ecological disaster, particularly through the over-exploitation of natural resources, man-made climate change, and the global dispersal of pollutants.

Conviviality

As I have already stated above, there is an alternative ethos:

conviviality. Ivan Illich, the South American philosopher, introduced the term in his book *Tools for Conviviality* (1973), and I have tried to develop it, including ideas from E.F. Schumacher's *Small is Beautiful* (1973), so that the adjective 'convivial' and the noun 'conviviality' are given a profound meaning which goes far beyond the jovial to identify the roots of human joy and the essence of humanity.

'Conviviality' is a way of living through which people gain quality of life and enjoy happiness by striving to be in harmony with themselves and with their social, cultural and natural environments. For each individual this can be a lifelong learning project; for every society it can be the source of peace, prosperity and sustainability.

Convivial people seek a state of deep and satisfying harmony with their world and through this a worthwhile and joyful meaning to their lives.

- Looking for harmony with their natural environment, they use it for their needs, but try not to exploit it; they strive to conserve the land and the living things which it supports and, seeing themselves as stewards, aim to safeguard the land for future generations.
- Looking for harmony with their cultural environment, they learn from it, savour it, contribute to it, and aim to pass on what they see as worthwhile to future generations.
- Seeking harmony with their fellows, convivial people try to cooperate rather than compete with them; they endeavour neither to exploit others nor to be exploited by them; they participate in the management of their society through democratic structures; they strive to live in concord with all – to love and be loved.
- Seeking harmony with their inner selves, convivial people search for understanding of their own rationality, spirituality

and emotions in order to develop their talents effectively, and by trying to use their talents harmoniously in relation to society and the environment, they experience the joy of convivial life.

Set out like that it is clear that conviviality is not an impossible ethos suggested by would-be do-gooders! In the tranquillity of their own homes most people will say 'amen' to these points. They will say 'Yes, we see these as worthwhile ideas, even if, from time to time, as does everybody, we fall short of achieving them.' There is nothing alien or wrong-headed here.

The fact is that in the micro-world of families and small communities, conviviality is usually the prevailing ethos. It is unspoken, but nevertheless in such groups, people mostly live in altruistic harmony with each other, supporting each other, conserving their surroundings and aiming to pass on to future generations that which they hold worthwhile.

Likewise, most teachers, doctors, nurses, social workers, charity workers, and carers for the elderly and sick, together with some lawyers, reflect the ethos of conviviality. In their professional contacts they support, not exploit, those who are dependent on them, and by the same token they aim to work in harmony with their colleagues.

Conviviality as a fundamental part of educating for the inevitable

So, what is the role of teachers in this? Can it be to ensure that the next generation recognises that convivial futures will be better than ones based on wealth creation and economic growth? Or, if that seems too directive, at least to ensure that the next generation sees that conviviality is a viable alternative to wealth creation?

Inevitably this means that teachers need to become significant contributors to political discussion in the classroom. This is something that teachers have always been warned against. But in the face of what I have described as inevitable, it should be seen as a dereliction of duty not to discuss relevant political issues as part of schooling.

When teachers were autonomous in their classrooms such a view would have had obvious dangers, but in the collegial schools argued for in this book, where what is taught is a matter for the teachers to decide collegially, and involves governors and others, an effective future-looking curriculum should be forged in every school.

How conviviality impinges on democratic politics

Democratic politics is a process through which people try to make collective decisions about the management of their affairs, local, national and worldwide.

Here are some of the major ways in which conviviality impinges on politics:

- *Tackling global warming* is a convivial issue because conviviality entails trying to safeguard the Earth for future generations and conserving it and the living things which it supports. It follows that rich countries must limit consumerism and replace economic growth by concern for the quality of life and the well-being of all.
- *Tackling poverty and malnutrition* wherever it exists is a convivial issue because conviviality entails seeking to live in harmony with fellow human beings and so supporting those in need. It follows that poor countries need to be able to grow their economies – aiming eventually to converge with the reduced economies of the presently rich

countries. This also gives a convivial reason for supporting fair trade.

- *Aiming for nations to be more or less self-sustainable in food production, energy provision, water availability and other natural resources* arises as a convivial issue because conviviality entails using the natural environment for needs, but not exploiting it; it involves conserving the land, and having stewardship of precious resources to safeguard future generations' access to these.

- *Aiming to avoid or reduce conflict* arises as a convivial issue because conviviality embraces the idea of harmony between peoples, the notion of all of us trying to cooperate rather than compete with each other, and of no one either exploiting or being exploited. This ideal stretches from in-family feuds and workplace bullying to terrorism and international warfare.

- *Aiming to replace individualism by community involvement* arises because conviviality includes the idea of harmony with fellows, and cooperation rather than competition. It embraces altruism.

- *Aiming to reduce inequality* arises as a convivial issue because conviviality endeavours neither to exploit others nor to be exploited by them and embraces democratic ideals of social justice as fundamental aspects of harmony between people. For these same reasons the convivial ethos embraces values of honesty, respect and empathy for others.

- *Espousing education which embraces notions of nurture, culture and survival and is convivial, worthwhile, satisfying, joyful and lifelong* arises from the notion that conviviality embraces harmony with one's cultural environment and learning from it, savouring it, contributing to it and aiming to pass on what is seen as worthwhile to future generations; and from the notion of seeking harmony with one's inner self and searching for understanding of one's rationality, spirituality and emotions in order to develop one's talents and lead a convivial life.

A worldwide viable future in which economies converge

These ideas are key to seeing how a viable global future could evolve. Our descendants across the globe – children, grandchildren and beyond – must be able to enjoy what they will perceive as a worthwhile quality of life. To achieve this, the convivial argument is that the industrial countries of the world should begin to replace the ethos of wealth creation by the ethos of conviviality in national and international life, while the developing countries should use wealth creation to raise the standards of living of their peoples and use conviviality to ensure that these standards are shared by all of them. Thus, rich economies should contract and poor economies expand to the point where they converge.

In order to succeed in this just mission it needs to be recognised that economic growth (i.e. wealth creation) is a phenomenon of societies moving to maturity, and thereafter economic stability (i.e. zero economic growth) is needed within societies which are convivial, and this is achieved by their being socially just, democratically governed, environmentally responsible, and culturally stimulating, and prospering mainly on the renewable resources and produce of their own territories, while trading minimally with each other and supporting one another in times of need.

Combating global warming is the greatest worldwide challenge of today, but it cannot be tackled in isolation from issues of malnutrition, poverty, resource depletion, economic growth, over-consumption, international trade, and sustainability. These are all relevant to creating a better world. A better world would avoid wars, famines, and eco-catastrophes. It would celebrate the cultural heritages of its peoples, ensure social justice for all, and focus its technological advances on ensuring the sustainability of life on Earth.

The essential role of teachers

As humankind becomes wealthier, in order to survive it must begin to eschew the pursuit of further wealth and instead seek quality of life for all. If we put the natural conviviality of people together with the reality of political action, progress just might be made towards sustainable, peaceful and just societies throughout the world.

Essentially, this is an uncompromising, earth-moving task for teachers – because fundamentally it is an educational issue. We all, adults and children, have to learn to live together on a small planet with finite resources.

9

Learning For When the Oil Runs Out

'Peak oil' and the need for cultural reform or dire consequences

The subtitle of this book, 'Schooling When the Oil Runs Out', is both a likely reality in terms of oil supplies becoming prohibitively expensive and a metaphor for other catastrophes that may hit global society. I have chosen not to expend print on these other matters, but rather to assume that the world of my grandchildren's generation will experience grave global problems. There are plenty of 'apocalyptic' writings – but virtually nothing on the kind of schooling that will have helped when the awful – whatever that may be – happens. But in justice to my subtitle, a quote from the website of *Energy Bulletin*, entitled *Peak Oil Primer*,[1] seems appropriate:

> *Peak oil* is the simplest label for … the peak in global oil production… Once we have used up about half of the original reserves, oil production becomes ever more likely to stop growing and begin a terminal decline, hence 'peak'. The peak in oil production does not signify 'running out of oil', but it does mean the end of cheap oil, as we

[1] http://www.energybulletin.net/primer.php

switch from a buyers' to a sellers' market. For economies leveraged on ever increasing quantities of cheap oil, the consequences may be dire. Without significant successful cultural reform, severe economic and social consequences seem inevitable... Our industrial societies and our financial systems were built on the assumption of continual growth – growth based on ever more readily available cheap fossil fuels. Oil in particular is the most convenient and multi-purposed of these fossil fuels. Oil currently accounts for about 43% of the world's total fuel consumption, and 95% of global energy used for transportation. Oil and gas are feedstocks for plastics, paints, pharmaceuticals, fertilizers, electronic components, tyres and much more. Oil is so important that the peak will have vast implications across the realms of war and geopolitics, medicine, culture, transport and trade, economic stability and food production... For certain tasks, such as air travel, no other energy source can readily be substituted for oil in large quantities.

So, what is an appropriate answer in terms of schooling today's children? Can the same answer be developed for adult education?

Education for creating sustainable ways of living

One summer a few years back I was teaching in Finland at the Rantasalmi Environmental Education Centre with Pekka Hynninen (Director of the Centre) and Professor Mauri Åhlberg of the University of Joensuu. We developed an educational model for students learning to create sustainable ways of life, as shown in Figure 3. The model shows how the processes of learning need to be integrated and cumulative if they are to lead to creating sustainable, and, hopefully, good-quality and satisfying ways of life. The model uses Åhlberg's approach to concept maps, whereby, as in the next paragraph, one should be able to read the diagram as prose and so garner its meaning.

For their survival, young people need to develop cognitive skills, environmental and social sensitivities, and civic skills. Cognitive skills and environmental sensitivity are needed for gaining environmental understanding. In addition, environmental and social sensitivities are needed in order to acquire and develop convivial values. Convivial values and environmental understanding, as well as cognitive skills are needed in order to engage in critical reflection on society's actions. Civic and cognitive skills are needed for students to acquire empowerment to act, and this is needed, in conjunction with critical reflection, in order to take steps to achieve a sustainable way of life. This holistic view is completed by recognising that a sustainable way of life is needed for the survival of life. It needs to be taught in the context of concern for the quality of life, and so should be learned with joy and not through drudgery.

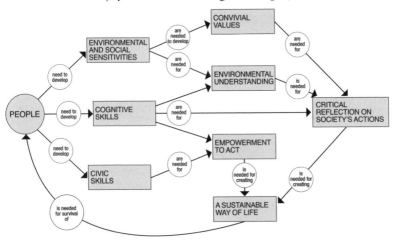

Figure 3. A concept map of education for survival

Survival needs cognitive skills

The acquisition of cognitive skills is a part of normal schooling; here, it is taken to include reading, writing, talking, listening, thinking, analysis, critique, synthesis, and creativity, as well as mathematical competence and statistical understanding.

Survival needs environmental and social sensitivities

The deliberate development of environmental sensitivity is sometimes, but not often, a part of present-day schooling. It is about valuing nature for its own sake: savouring rain and sunshine, forest and field, butterfly and sparrow, rocks and streams. For some it comes from early childhood visits 'into the country' with parents, or through camping and hiking with scouts or guides, or from the acquisition of a garden and the need to tend it.

My late colleague Malcolm Plant argued in his book *Education for the Environment*[1] that 'favourable childhood experiences spent in nature are a basis for cherishing this identity with nature in later life', and he noted how George Eliot in *The Mill on the Floss* beautifully captured this idea in these words:

> We could never have loved the earth so well if we had had no childhood in it... What novelty is worth that sweet monotony where everything is known and loved because it is known?

There is good research evidence, as Plant shows, that childhood experience of nature can be a significant factor in the development of personal commitment to the environment. So when we try

---

[1] Malcolm Plant, *Education for the Environment: Stimulating Practice* (Dereham: Peter Francis, 1998).

to prepare young people to strive for a sustainable world, we need to ensure that they get this kind of experience in suitable abundance.

Schools, particularly those in urban areas, need to organise regular visits and expeditions into the countryside. In England some do at present, but the demands of the National Curriculum and assessment and inspection impede the practice. In Scandinavia, perhaps because of the rigours of the winter climate, schools are more geared to the surrounding countryside.

Likewise, young people need to learn to savour their cultural environment: the literature, arts, sciences, heritage, and ideas that abound and are accessible to all who choose to seek them. Schools are often more focused on this than on the natural environment. Involvement in both the natural and cultural environments matters in order that children, and the adults they grow into, learn to enjoy and revere things rather than persistently seek out and squeak at the next thrill. It is the antidote to boredom.

The development of social sensitivity is equally necessary. This includes the awareness that others are people with feelings like ourselves and deserve to be respected as fellow human beings. Schools are usually well versed in this aspect of education.

Survival needs civic skills

Civic skills overlap with the cognitive skills, but go beyond them in being the ability to marshal arguments, formulate questions, 'think on one's feet', and make a case, with clarity and civility, in a civic setting such as a school debate, a community meeting, or a public enquiry.

Survival needs environmental understanding

Environmental understanding embraces the chemistry, physics, biology, ecology, mathematics, geography, geology, psychology, sociology, economics, history, philosophy, and so on that impinge on natural and social environmental issues. These disciplines are part of the academic culture of our time. In the terms of this book, in cases where schools are collegial, what is taught depends upon local decisions; the extent to which these disciplines are taught, and to whom, depends upon the teachers and on their own environmental understanding. These disciplines are, of course, part of the magnificence of our intellectual heritage, and the better that anyone is versed in them, the greater their concept of the path to sustainability.

Survival needs conviviality

In Chapter 8 I elaborated a green coherent moral vision called 'conviviality'. It encompasses the environmentally and socially oriented values that many teachers subscribe to, and which I believe are needed if the world is to survive as a habitat for humankind.

To repeat what is said in that chapter, conviviality has a profound meaning concerned with the nature of life. A convivial person is trying to achieve a state of deep and satisfying harmony with the world, which gives joyful meaning to life. Convivial people are striving for harmony with their environment, their fellows and their self.

How do people develop such values? To require a particular set to be learned and used to underpin actions is considered by teachers to be indoctrination, and is properly rejected by them. Instead, the educational approach is to enable children to grow up in a climate where particular values are held by those whom the children respect, and for the children slowly to be encouraged to acquire similar values. This is why the values held by teachers are important, and why the activities referred to under the heading of environmental and social sensitivity are vital.

There is a terrible tension between these convivial values and the hedonistic and acquisitive values of consumerist capitalism, where exploiting the riches of the Earth and the labour of others is not only seen as acceptable but is lauded. Rampant consumerism, pursued by millions of people, is damaging the Earth by polluting it and causing it to overheat. Strangely, most people individually subscribe to convivial values in some form, yet en masse pursue hedonistic and acquisitive goals. As argued in the previous chapter, the hope is that education can, in a phrase, turn the heat down.

Survival needs critical reflection on society's actions

Everybody who recognises changes in the annual weather pattern can engage in a debate on climate change. The ill-informed can simply disregard the scientific evidence of global warming or its causes or its likely consequences. The same applies to those who are so blinkered with their own affluence and its growth that they put everything else to one side. Those who recognise the scientific evidence but who embrace the view that each generation must solve its own problems will want to take no action. And for nearly all of us who understand the issue and have environmentally friendly values, myself included, there is the utter inertia of feeling that anything we can do is of such minor consequence that it is not worth putting ourselves out to do it. This is when we need empowerment. It is something that people should learn at school and develop throughout their lives.

Survival needs empowerment to act

Most people are reluctant to put their heads above the parapet. There is a common reluctance to speak out. Empowerment to act is about helping people to speak their mind. Empowerment is about giving people the self-confidence to strive for what they believe in: the courage to stand up and argue the case for something that matters.

Empowerment is cumulative: one successful experience encourages the next and reinforces the view that active citizenship can make things better. It is only learned experientially.

In England, the government encourages schools to reduce car use in getting children to school. As with most government actions, it is a top-down initiative. Suppose that instead it became a bottom-up development, with classes in primary schools in England taking it on as a project. It would require skilled and courageous teaching to guide and support the children. Suppose that the children monitored how many people travelled to and from their school by car, calculated how much petrol is turned into carbon dioxide, and campaigned to reduce car use by getting more children to walk – along safe routes – to and from school. Suppose they succeeded in reducing car usage and invited the local press to report on their project. These children would know that they had begun to tackle global warming and would learn that well-orchestrated campaigns can work. It would empower them to continue.

Perhaps next, and more difficult because of the commercial implications, they might begin to campaign with their families to buy more locally grown food and so help reduce the consumption of fossil fuels in intercontinental food transport. Undoubtedly such campaigns would cause friction with the business world because of a clash between business ethics (based on profit and power) and school ethics (based on environment and community); but this is the battlefield on which all of our futures depend. Suppose that schools put reports of their ecological campaigns on school web pages on the Internet. Suppose that they began to email schools around the world, urging them also to campaign.

I know that many will say that children should not be embroiled in this kind of activity. But this is to fail to understand that the children's world is seriously threatened, and so it is right that their education should empower them to strive to protect it.

Empowerment is potentially dangerous. It needs to be community-focused and not consumer-based. This is why the fostering of environmental and social sensitivity and the development of convivial values must be its educational precursors.

Survival needs a sustainable way of life

The aim is that critical reflection on society's actions, coupled with the empowering experience of the kind of campaigns described above, prepares the next generation for comprehending, hopefully coping with, and ultimately reducing life-threatening environmental change. In part these reductions can come from individual actions, but most will be achieved by legislation: in the democracies of the world, such legislation is crucially dependent on the electorate understanding and accepting the need for tough measures.

That is a rationale for the kind of education for survival described here. Fundamentally it overarches the present governmental drives to raise standards of literacy and numeracy in schools: these should be recognised as just one of the tools needed for the future.

Governments throughout the world are trying to reduce their

carbon footprints. What are the consequences for the large number of people whose work entails carbon dioxide production, and who thereby become unemployed – those in the transport industries engaged in moving goods across the world (and burning fossil fuel to do it), and those who mass-grow the food or manufacture the goods which are transported, for example?

The answer, in terms of employment for these people, is that food growing and goods production need to become more local and, using what Schumacher in *Small is Beautiful* called 'intermediate technology', more labour intensive. Eddie Gallagher, once chief executive of the Environment Agency, said: 'Stand on a bridge on the M1 and count the biscuit lorries travelling north and the biscuit lorries travelling south: you'll find there are hundreds of them, the counts are the same, and they are all full of biscuits.'

Can't Edinburgh shortbread destined to be eaten in London be made there?

A hundred and fifty years ago, and still today in many parts of the world, a large proportion of the population grew most of its own food and made with its own hands some of the domestic goods that were needed. We will probably need to do the same in the future. If we decided to, we certainly could do it, and with much greater surety of success than in the past because of the scientific and technological knowledge now available. The starting point for the mind shift and the necessary skills should be school.

Ecology of the future versus economy of the past

An account of education based on ecological survival is a far cry from what governments today see as required. But sadly, ruling establishments which couldn't foresee the recent crash of the global economy, still have not seen how imperative it is that our young people are prepared for the daunting ecology of the future and not the failing economy of the past. But these young people's parents' generation needs also to be involved, which is why in Chapter 1 I argued that the press needs to embrace responsibility for adult education.

10

Re-thinking Secondary Education in England

Thirteen years of early life locked in a classroom

The legal requirement that every young person, from age 5 to age 16 – and from 2013, to age 18 – must be incarcerated in a school classroom with up to 30 other youngsters for some five hours every week day, for some forty weeks of every year, working at the behest of a sequence of teachers who are expected to make every forty-minute lesson stimulating, meaningful and valuable to everyone in the class, would be beyond belief – except for the fact that we all experienced it when we were young.

Primary schools

Primary school children are usually biddable: mostly they accept adult authority and, with good teaching, they are often enthusiastic about school. The class system, with one generalist teacher for most of the time for a school year, with occasional specialist support, usually works well for these younger children. Once the primary schools are freed from the constraints currently imposed by government and able to work collegially in the way described in Chapter 4, it will be up to the teachers, governors, parents and local community to ensure that every primary school is a good school and responds effectively to the educational needs of the children. Professor Robin Alexander's Cambridge Primary Review, entitled *Children, Their World, Their Education* (2010), and Professor Richard Layard and Judy Dunn's *A Good Childhood* (2009) will no doubt become the standard works for primary school teachers' collegial reflections on their work.

Secondary schools

But finding the path for all secondary schools to be good schools is more problematic. Young people in their teens, nowadays termed 'students', can be difficult. As they become fully physically mature, but emotionally are still developing, they can be a challenge to anyone who is in authority over them. Many students enjoy academic study and a few relish examinations, but most don't. Some are utterly bored by schooling and learn that most dangerous of skills – how to switch off from what's going on around them. (Why do so many people not vote at elections? Perhaps it is because at school they learned to avoid the injunction, 'Pay attention, this is important').

Compared with the schooling of former times, the task of teaching is much harder today. The pressures on teachers, particularly in secondary schools, are more demanding, even though many of them are more highly skilled at teaching. Young people are more likely to be truculent and difficult to control, perhaps because the pleasures and distractions of their lives outside school are much greater in terms of portable music, easy communication with mobile phones, computer games, relaxed sexual mores, and easy access to illicit substances, including alcohol. And now schooling for all is to be extended to age 18.

Before considering what the future could offer, it is salient to examine some of the structural developments in secondary education introduced by recent governments in England.

Politics enters schools

As noted in Chapter 6, in the 1980s government in England became increasingly concerned about what was happening to young people during the years of compulsory education, and ever since 1988, administrations of the right and the left have tried to raise standards of attainment for school leavers by making changes in the education system. Sadly, innovations have tended to focus on the basic skills that business and industrial employers consider lacking in their new recruits, and so educational ideas based on a broad and balanced curriculum have tended to become subservient to political concerns about the economy.

Starting in 1988, national government has constantly tinkered with education. Twelve secretaries of state and countless junior ministers have tried to demonstrate their political ability (and aspirations for higher office) by introducing parliamentary education bills and sending a myriad of regulations to schools.[1] This continues to happen notwithstanding strong concerns expressed by teachers' unions, individual teachers and heads, academic researchers and various public figures that these have become counterproductive. Central control of education is overwhelming the schools with bureaucracy and restricting the opportunities for teachers to teach creatively in relation to the educational needs

---

[1] In 2006, 192 new initiatives were sent to schools; in 2007, the figure was 242.

of their pupils. Nevertheless, many schools still manage to provide exceptional experiences of lasting value for their pupils. Would that they all could.

Conservative Government interventions, 1988–1997

Response to public concern

Whether public concern triggered political action, or whether it was the other way round, is arguable. What is certain is that in the 1970s and 1980s, in some of the schools in deprived communities, where there were few employment prospects for school leavers, some of the teachers considered that happiness in the classroom was better than hard-grind learning for jobs that didn't exist. It may have led to laissez-faire attitudes to work. In other schools, teachers embraced a fashion that said that spelling and punctuation didn't matter as much as an ability to create and communicate, nor did arithmetic matter with the advent of pocket calculators and electronic tills in shops. Widespread also was the lack of recognition by most teachers that regular assessment to see what has been learned by each individual is an essential part of effective education. These all came to a head when business leaders and industrialists began to criticise the lack of basic skills and the poor attitudes to work of school leavers, and expressed fears that our future economic prosperity was at risk. Politicians had to respond and, as noted in Chapter 6, their first major intervention into 'the secret garden of the curriculum' was the Education Reform Act of 1988, when Kenneth Baker was Education Secretary and Margaret Thatcher Prime Minister. Nearly every year since then has seen the grip of the state on education tighten.

Local authorities criticised

In 1902 local education authorities were created, and until 1988 they had overall responsibility for ensuring that there were enough state school places for the children in each area, as well as for the financial administration of state schools, for the upkeep of school buildings and grounds, and for appointing teachers and head teachers.[1] Central government provided most of the funding, but county councils and city councils in many cases augmented this, particularly in support of local building or special curriculum projects. Notionally the local authorities were responsible for the curriculum of their schools, but in practice the schools, and teachers within the schools, were autonomous in designing and teaching courses that led to the various awards of the free-standing, university-influenced examination boards. But when, in the 1980s, as noted in the above paragraph, there was widespread criticism of schooling, it was the local authorities who seemed to take the blame.

The Education Reform Act of 1988 and its political consequences

The Education Reform Act of 1988 made some crucial changes in the education system. It took the financial administration of schools away from local authorities and delegated it to schools' governing bodies. Local Management of Schools (LMS) enabled schools (or, strictly, governors' finance committees) to decide within their allocated budget how much to spend on equipment, materials and buildings and, within legal limits, whether to increase or reduce staffing.

Under this act, parents were entitled to a choice of schools

---

[1] For the sake of brevity I have omitted the 'voluntary-aided' schools where the Church owns the buildings and appoints most of the governing body but the State pays the teachers.

rather than the one which the local authority had designated for their children (in a sequence of measures which became increasingly tortuous). It also replaced the notional local control of what was taught in schools with a highly prescriptive subject-based curriculum for all young people aged 5 to 16 (the 'National Curriculum'), and introduced nationwide external testing of young people at 7, 11 and 14, with the averaged results for each school published in league tables (in order to assist parents in choosing schools). Four years later, the Office for Standards in Education (Ofsted) was established and began regular, systematic and searching inspections of schools aimed to raise standards of attainment and to ensure that government policies were being fully implemented.

It was a necessary jolt to teaching, and once some of the teething troubles (such as the obsessive detail of the first design of the National Curriculum) were overcome, standards in schools improved. While results in England for 11-year-olds' Sats climbed until 2005 and then more or less levelled, results at GCSE (where the desired outcome was at least five at grades A*-C) continue to climb slowly, as shown in Figure 4.

Figure 4   Percentage of 15-year-olds achieving 5 or more A*–C at GCSE

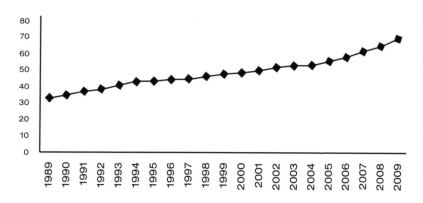

The government, of course, claimed the credit for this, while the opposition criticised it for not achieving more. Yet surely it is the young people and their teachers who deserve the credit. The worry is, however, that the curriculum has narrowed towards the things that are measured. It is likely that the accelerated increase from 2007 is due to schools becoming streetwise on how to maximise results – there are allegations of schools concentrating teaching efforts on the C/D boundary, of encouraging students to take 'softer' GCSE subjects, and even of offering prize money to successful students. Soon, as has happened with primary school assessments, the graph will flatten: not everybody is academically able to achieve what is actually quite a demanding result.

Labour Government interventions, 1997–2010

Treasure hunts for pots of gold

When Labour came to power in 1997, as noted in Chapter 6, Tony Blair famously proclaimed the key policy of 'education, education, education'. More money was put into education, but instead of concentrating it in schools where there was the greatest need, treasure hunts were set up so that schools bid for pots of gold deposited by ministers for their pet ideas. It was part of the mantra of 'choice' whereby it was envisaged that, with parents having a choice of schools with different strengths, market forces would operate, and to survive the competition, schools would raise their standards.

Whereas many on the left wing of the Labour party had hoped the government would abolish grammar schools and strengthen the comprehensive system, this did not happen. When Alastair Campbell, press adviser to Prime Minister Tony

Blair, referred to 'bog-standard comprehensive schools', there was despair about Labour's plans for secondary education.

Comprehensives turn into specialist schools

One of the most curious political ventures was inviting comprehensive schools to bid for specialist school status. A secondary school could seek extra funding for one subject, or sometimes two, which, while still meeting the overall requirements of the National Curriculum, would 'provide enriched learning opportunities' in the specialism. Provided that it could raise £50,000 in sponsorship, the school could bid for £100,000 from the government for a capital project and, if successful, it would get a recurrent fund of £129 per pupil per year for up to 1,000 pupils for three years to 'implement their specialist school development plan'. According to the Department for Children, Schools and Families website (in early 2010), this 'helps schools to establish distinctive identities through their chosen specialisms and achieve their targets to raise standards'.

In December 2009 the government website said that there were 2,502 designated specialist schools, including 583 in technology, 408 in arts, 354 in sports, 282 in science, 222 in mathematics and computing and 217 in business and enterprise. Since there were only 3,100 state secondary schools in England, it looks as though nearly every school had become specialist. Giving this enhanced status and funding to what presumably would already be the strongest departments (as put forward by the schools), rather than to departments which were struggling, seems like 'it's the rich who get the gravy and the poor who get the blame'.

Part of the rhetoric in favour of this policy was that it helped parents choose a school which they thought would benefit their child because of its specialism. It is a dubious argument: at age eleven, only rarely is it clear – to the parents or the child – in what direction a child may develop; the choice of specialisms within the travelling distance of the parental home is likely to be limited except in dense urban areas; and it is unclear how far the school's emphasis on the specialism will benefit the individual child.

Creation of academies

A later bizarre form of funding introduced by the Labour government was the academy programme. This is how the Department for Children, Schools and Families[1] described it in December 2009:

> Academies are all-ability, state-funded schools established and managed by sponsors... Sponsors challenge traditional thinking on how schools are run and what they should be like for students. They seek to make a complete break with cultures of low aspiration which afflict too many communities and their schools... Academies are funded at a level comparable to other local schools in the area.
>
> The governing body and the headteacher have responsibility for managing the academy. In order to determine the ethos and leadership of the academy, and ensure clear responsibility and accountability, the private sector or charitable sponsor always appoints the majority of the governors. All academies are bound by the same School Admission Code, SEN Code of Practice and exclusions guidance as all other state-funded schools. All new Academies are also required to follow the national curriculum programmes of study in English, maths, science and ICT.

---

[1] A Labour administration.

All have specialist school status and have a specialism in one or more subjects.

It was, of course, an excellent idea to put additional funding into education in socially deprived areas where there was 'a culture of low aspiration', but why did this have to be run by business people and charities rather than by the existing local authorities? It certainly led to some undesirable controversy when evangelical Christians from the private sector began to exert an influence on the teaching of evolution in their academies.

Under the heading 'Why Academies?', in December 2009 the department's website explained:

> Academies are a key element of the drive to raise standards; raising aspirations and creating opportunities in some of the most disadvantaged communities in the country. Academies have a mission to transform education where the status quo is simply not good enough. We want academies to be the engine of social mobility... Most academies replace existing underperforming schools... Academies will help break the cycle of underachievement in areas of social and economic deprivation whether in inner cities, suburban or rural areas. Each Academy will offer local solutions for local needs.

The early academies were set up by the Labour administration when Ed Balls was Secretary of State. In many of the two hundred established, it seems to have gone something like this. In a socially deprived neighbourhood a struggling comprehensive school was identified where, however committed the teachers were, and however hard they worked, examination results at GCSE were well below the national average. Because the results were low, and possibly for other reasons, Ofsted put the school into 'special measures'. A sponsor was found to take over the school (originally this sponsor was expected to provide £2 million, but this was later waived), and the costs of building a new architect-designed new school or entirely refurbishing the old buildings were mainly or entirely met by central government. The governing body and the head teacher (as appointed by the local authority) were sacked. A new governing body was appointed, mainly by the sponsor, and a new head teacher – now called 'the principal' – was appointed. The old school was closed and the staff encouraged to apply to be interviewed for work at the new academy – probably under different conditions of service, devised by the private-sector sponsors. The pupils were given the option of transferring to the new academy. The principal, senior managers and governors developed a new curriculum (within the government's constraints noted above) 'to meet the needs of the individual pupils in their school'.

In a wonderful expression of enthusiasm (without a shred of explanation as to how it would happen), the department's website, in December 2009, said:

> The outcomes expected are not simply good examination results but also young people superbly equipped for active citizenship: committed to lifelong learning; and, ready for progression into further and higher education and work.

Academies sounded promising and exciting, except to those who may have thought about it like this: same kids, same teachers, same social environment. If refurbished buildings, a new head, and redesigned curriculum is all that was needed, why all the ballyhoo? Why give power to run the school to non-paying sponsors (an oxymoron, surely?) whose business ethos, academic status or religious fervour are unlikely to be accompanied by an educational understanding of the holistic experience that young people need. Why wasn't this power given to the previous head, teachers and governors?

Labour planned to create another two hundred such academies – but lost the general election of May 2010.

Raising the school leaving age

In June 2007 the Labour government announced that from 2013 everyone's formal education would be continued to age 18. Students would either continue at school with academic studies, transfer to a further education college for vocational studies, or take an apprenticeship with a company that gave a guaranteed minimum training. This was aimed at reducing youth unemployment and ensuring that more people gained the skills demanded of industry. The Conservative/Lib-Dem coalition government is keeping to this plan.

Conservative/Lib-Dem Coalition Government interventions, 2010–

Within six months of the new administration, Michael Gove, Secretary of State in the now renamed Department of Education, drastically cut the schools building programme of the previous administration, set up procedures for parent-led 'free schools' and radically changed the academy programme. Whereas Labour was trying to turn around failing schools with the academy programme, the new government invited all schools top-rated by Ofsted (i.e. those described as 'outstanding') to apply for academy status. At the same time, the new administration slightly enhanced the income of schools with children from deprived homes with a modest 'pupil premium'.

Worryingly, Gove is looking towards paying teachers according to their classroom performance. He is preparing the ground for a new national curriculum, having abolished the quango that was responsible for the old one. Critics say he is trying to reproduce the privileged education that he received as a schoolboy. He has reset the target for GCSE results as five A*–C grades in English, mathematics, a science, a language and either history or geography, and called this the 'English Baccalaureate', and thus played down the value of the variety of other subjects offered by schools.

In January 2011 he announced that a new national curriculum will be drawn up. He said:

> We have sunk in international league tables and the National Curriculum is substandard. Meanwhile the pace of economic and technological change is accelerating and our children are being left behind. The previous curriculum failed to prepare us for the future. We must change course. Our review will examine the best school systems in the world and give us a world-class curriculum that will help teachers, parents and children know what children should learn at what age.[1]

I fear the auguries are not good: he has not given any indication that he understands the issues with which this book is concerned. He is thinking only within the frame of 'business as usual', and of the economic system competing with the rest of the world.

So, what *should* a good secondary school look like? Here are six pointers:

---

[1] http://www.sustainablegov.co.uk/education/michael-gove-announces-major-review-of-national-curriculum (26 January 2011).

1. A good secondary school should be depoliticised

First, as argued in Chapter 6, it is necessary to take government out of schooling. Education must be depoliticised – taken out of party politics. Ofsted must be replaced by more effective methods of evaluation and accountability based on schools, their governors and their localities. League tables must be abandoned. Testing before the end of schooling should be the province of teachers – guided but not controlled by government. Ministers must stop meddling and imposing new initiatives. Teachers must be trusted, within collegially organised schools, to teach according to their professional judgements concerning the educational needs of their students.

2. A good secondary school should be local

Second, as argued in Chapter 5, secondary schools (like primary schools) need to be local. Students need to be able to cycle or walk to school. Perhaps catchment areas might be based on the catchment areas of three or four primary schools. This is an important part of building vibrant communities – as Diane Ravitch has recognised in the United States (see Chapter 5).

A problem, of course, for faith schools is that either they will have to lose their religious affiliation and become neighbourhood schools fitting into the geography of the local catchment areas, or slowly lose their pupils when the local schools are recognised as good schools. Likewise, the grammar schools and the various schools set up by other bodies will need to move into the new system and become neighbourhood schools with locally elected governors. This will be a difficult nettle for Parliament to grasp. However, once it is politically recognised that local, neighbourhood schools, collegially organised and with the accountability structure discussed in this book, provide the best route both to excellent education for all and to community development (as ecology replaces economy as the political driving force), it will be easier. Who pays the piper calls the tune, and it is, of course, Parliament that votes the money that is available for the present range of comprehensive schools, grammar schools, faith schools, academies, free schools and so on. In other words, Parliament can grasp the nettle and turn every secondary state-funded school into a local, neighbourhood school. Perhaps the term 'academy' should be used for every local secondary school, and 'school' reserved for primary schools.

3. A good secondary school should not be too large

Third, they must not be too large. Ideally, perhaps secondary schools should have around 500 students and 30 staff in order that both students and staff have a chance of knowing and being known by most of their fellows. As most educationists, but few politicians, realise, learning is for most people primarily a social activity. Some personal knowledge of those with whom one is working is an important contributor to learning with them.

In urban areas it may be that the idea of middle schools should be re-introduced, that students aged 11 to 13 attend for three years, going on to high school for four years, from 14 to 18 years old (i.e. now that the leaving age is to be raised to 18). This would avoid having large schools, although on the down side it might frustrate some of the teachers who enjoy working across the range of ages. The pairing of middle and high schools might facilitate teachers moving at the end of a year to another age range – which, of course, is what can happen in primary schools.

4. A good secondary school should be collegial and self-determining

Fourth, the staff should work collegially (as described in Chapter 4) to find ways in which the curriculum and teaching methods, taking into account the timetable and available space, can focus on nurture, culture and survival, in ways which will be purposeful and enjoyable for all of their students.

In terms of *nurture*, it should be seen as essential that every student has one key figure – a teacher – who has oversight of their school life, and to whom they can relate personally and with mutual respect, perhaps for a year, or for the whole of the period they are in the school. Hopefully the concept of conviviality would underpin this focus – as described in Chapter 8.

In terms of *culture*, the teachers might consider the teaching union ATL's skills-based curriculum, Richard Pring's *Nuffield Review of 14–19 Education*, or David Hargreaves' 'systems redesign' as starting points, each of which are now outlined.

In 2009 the ATL published a booklet called *Subject to Change: New Thinking on the Curriculum*. It is one of the sources of inspiration that schools could adopt. In it, the authors write:

> We advocate a skills-based curriculum. One that is focused on communication, physical, interpersonal and intra-personal skills and thinking and learning skills: all essential components of the educated person able to think and act effectively in the twenty-first century.

Richard Pring's *Nuffield Review of 14–19 Education* is a similarly massive rethink of the traditional views about secondary education for older students. It

argues for an understanding of education for all which

would provide: the knowledge and understanding required for the 'intelligent management of life'; competence to make decisions about the future in the light of changing economic and social conditions; practical capability – including preparation for employment; moral seriousness with which to shape future choices and relationships; and a sense of responsibility for the community.

Perhaps even more fundamental are the ideas which David Hargreaves calls 'system redesign'. Peter Wilby (*Guardian*, 22 September 2009) described them as follows:

In Hargreaves' vision of 21st-century schooling, pupils help make the curriculum, tell the school how to use information technology, set standards and learning objectives, assess their own and one another's work, spend half or whole days on collaborative projects, sometimes work at home. Teachers are mentors or coaches who comment on students' work rather than grading it. Subjects become 'essential learnings', such as communication, thinking or social responsibility; or 'competencies', such as managing information or relating to people. Schools become part of networks, working with other schools or colleges, sometimes outsourcing even the work of whole departments...

He insists he doesn't have a blueprint. The impetus comes from below, from heads and teachers rethinking how we go about secondary education. He just pulled things together and helped them along, and the 23 pamphlets he has produced over the last four years quote numerous examples of mind-boggling innovations from the grassroots. 'We are not talking about a new model of schooling, handed down from above,' he says. 'The notion that there should be or can be a standard model is dead.'

In terms of *survival*, the ideas of Chapter 9 should be important, especially the notion that critical reflection on society's actions and empowerment to act are needed in order that the next generation can create a sustainable way of life.

5. GCSE and A-level examinations should be abolished

Fifth, abolish GCSE and A-level examinations. Provide end-of-schooling, externally assessed diplomas at 18+ to indicate to would-be employers or higher education admission tutors a student's academic and practical achievements. All other summative assessments, throughout schooling, should be made by teachers, moderated and guided as necessary, and from time to time communicated to both students and their parents.

Every school leaver, at 18+, should be given a comprehensive document profiling their various achievements – academic, vocational, sporting, creative, social, and so on. This, in a nutshell, is what *14–19 Curriculum and Qualifications Reform*, the far-sighted and comprehensive report of Mike Tomlinson and his working group, set out in October 2004. Shamefully, it was rejected by the Labour administration which had called for it.

Tomlinson did not peer into the future as this book does; he did not mention climate change or resource depletion. But in stark, powerful prose he saw the inadequacy of what we provide for 14+ students now:

> It is our view that the status quo is not an option. Nor do we believe further piecemeal changes are desirable. Too many young people leave education lacking basic and personal skills; our vocational provision is too fragmented; the burden of external assessment on learners, teachers

and lecturers is too great; and our system is not providing the stretch and challenge needed, particularly for high attainers. The results are a low staying-on rate post–16; employers having to spend large sums of money to teach the 'basics'; HE struggling to differentiate between top performers; and young people's motivation and engagement with education reducing as they move through the system.

Our report sets out a clear vision for a unified framework of 14–19 curriculum and qualifications. We want scholarship in subjects to be given room to flourish and we want high quality vocational provision to be available from age 14. These are different, but both, in their own terms, are vital to the future wellbeing of young people and hence our country. We want to bring back a passion for learning, and enable all learners to achieve as highly as possible and for their achievements to be recognised. We must ensure rigour and that all young people are equipped with the knowledge, skills and attributes needed for HE, employment and adult life.

I believe this is an excellent blueprint. The sooner we have a government with the courage to implement it, the better.

6. Community work and the parliamentary vote for young people are essential

Sixth, ensure that from 16 to 18 young people spend as much school time working in the local community as they do in the classroom or apprentice workshop. They must be trusted to act as responsible citizens. Give them the parliamentary vote.

The opportunities for teacher-led and student-led teams to engage in community work are tremendous: supporting elderly people, helping younger children in primary schools, growing vegetables, tending livestock, providing street theatre, enhancing local environments, erecting solar panels, planting trees, and through such teamwork learning democratic values and a convivial ethos based on harmony, co-operation, stewardship and self-sufficiency.

At the same time there must be good opportunities provided for the many who seek academic learning – while maintaining social coherence in the population of a school. In addition, there could be chances for school parties to go abroad on community missions.

Parliamentary action is needed

I have argued that politicians should leave education alone. The one structural task for Parliament should be to clear the decks so that secondary education can be based on the six points above.

Inept as the 2009 Copenhagen conference sadly proved to be, it gave out a clear message that life on this planet is going to get much tougher for everybody, and will be catastrophic for some at least. 'Business as usual' is not a viable option. Massive change in our society is inevitable and must be reflected in a new and vibrant approach to education. In England the mindset that economic prosperity will depend upon the business-friendly skills of school leavers should be seen to be ridiculous – it is how these young people embrace ecological sustainability and perhaps survival skills that will matter. That is the area on which Parliament should enable our schools to focus.

11

Educating Teachers for the Inevitable

The joy of teaching

To teach someone something that they did not know or could not do before is immensely satisfying – and virtually everybody can do it on a one-to-one basis if they are patient and the learner is willing. But to do it for several hours a day, five days a week, with 20 or 30 youngsters, is a task of a different magnitude – equally satisfying, but demanding personal energy, self-confidence, appropriate knowledge, insight into the development of young people, and pedagogic skill. For those who can do it successfully, teaching is a great job; for those who can't, it can be hell (both for them and for their pupils), and the sooner they leave it, the better.

Government pressures

Sadly, in recent years, the national governments in England – Conservative, Labour, and the Conservative/Lib-Dem coalition – have taken it upon themselves to control the classroom work of school teachers tightly. In terms of the National Curriculum, governments have told teachers what to teach; in certain areas of literacy and numeracy, they have told primary teachers exactly

157

how to teach; and for all teachers, they have dictated a tedious lesson format based on 'tell them what you're going to tell them, tell them it, and tell them what you've told them', and through processes of testing and inspection there are regular checks on the extent to which teachers are doing as they are told.

Although they would deny it, in effect governments have seen teachers as knowledge-transmitting and skills-training technicians who need to be given a manual and rule book in order to operate in a pupil factory and who need rigorous inspection and regular pupil assessment in order to ensure that they are working at maximum efficiency and obeying the employer's rules.

This micro-management has done enormous harm. It has damaged the spontaneity, the creativity and the flexibility in lessons that were once the hallmark of good practice in English schools. So, when Ofsted, Sats, the National Curriculum and league tables – the instruments of government control – have been swept away, as argued for in this book, what should we expect of teachers?

Teachers need to light fires, not fill pots

Obviously all teachers need substantial knowledge and understanding of whatever they are teaching and clear ideas on how to teach it. Beyond that, teachers need to be warm-hearted towards young people, as well as to have the personal skills to be able to maintain order and good discipline in the classroom, a task which can sometimes be very demanding. But there is much more to the work of school teachers if they are, as the poet Yeats put it (in a concept which can be traced back to the ancient Greeks, if not earlier), to 'light fires' in the minds of their pupils.

They need to have empathy and respect for young people and their parents. They need a sense of humour. They need to be able to inspire the young and generate enthusiasm which excites their pupils' imagination with ideas that will stay with them for years.

They need to have, variously, some of the attributes of creative artists, critical writers, inquisitive scientists, erudite librarians, puzzling mathematicians, performance musicians, well-read historians, dramatists, explorers, inventors, entrepreneurs, sports enthusiasts and more. Of course, no one can cover such a spectrum of interests in any depth.

Primary teachers need a broad coverage but can only be expected to excel in one or two areas. But if, as children move through primary school, one year they meet a class teacher with a bent for creative art, then the next year one who enjoys scientific enquiry in the classroom, and the next year someone skilled in drama, and so on, they are likely to find much inspiration to develop their varied talents. Every primary school teacher does, of course, need to be particularly skilled in the pedagogy of reading, writing and elementary mathematics.

Likewise, secondary school teachers need to be skilled in the pedagogy of reading and writing as well as in the essential specialism of a subject and its pedagogy. In addition, they need to be able to relate effectively to adolescents individually and en masse, and to respond with understanding to the mood changes, enthusiasms and worries of those in their teenage years.

Both primary and secondary teachers need to develop the skills of 'assessment for learning' which ensure that teaching is effectively geared to learning for every individual pupil.

Inspired teaching comes from people with 'fire in the belly'. While the classroom teacher must provide a variety of activities, as all parents will expect, the freedom to put emphasis on a personal strength will benefit many children. By comparison, a national curriculum, telling teachers year by year what they must teach, is often a recipe for boredom in both teachers and pupils. Likewise, a required pedagogy of how to teach, with a formalised beginning, middle and end to each lesson, carefully planned in writing beforehand – as currently expected by Ofsted – is a death sentence to spontaneity in the classroom.

There is one more quality needed of teachers: they need to 'walk tall' in society, to be respected by parents and the local community and recognised as people who, within the structure of a collegial school, can be trusted to provide the best education for the young people in their care. This will become increasingly important in the future, when schools become local and communities develop.

There is no higher calling

Demanding? Yes. Some may say that it asks too much. But others will recognise that it sets an aspiration for those who believe, as I do, that teachers have a fundamental role in our society. For, as the late Ted Wragg said, 'There is no higher calling. Without teachers, society would slide back into primitive squalor.'

Educating and training teachers

At present there are a bewildering number of routes into teaching:

- a first degree (3 or 4 years) followed by a postgraduate certificate, PGCE (1 year);

- a first degree (4 years) that includes teacher training – BA(Ed) or BEd;
- a first degree (3 or 4 years) followed by training in a school (either as a paid employee on the GTP (Graduate Teacher Programme) or as a student on a SCITT (School-Centred Initial Teacher Training) programme.

In the second half of the twentieth century teachers were trained either in universities on postgraduate certificate courses (mainly for secondary education), or in training colleges, renamed as colleges of education, absorbed into polytechnics as departments of education, and then converted into departments of education in the new universities. In the latter, two-year certificate courses were upgraded to three years, then to four-year bachelor degrees, while postgraduate certificate courses also started up in these institutions.

Courses varied. Some had good reputations, others did not. Critics complained that courses were too academic and an ineffective training for the reality of schools. The typical diet of psychology, sociology, philosophy and history of education was held to lack the all-important study of pedagogy. Some teacher trainers were excellent and a source of welcome new ideas into schools; others were dire, leading to the pejorative view that 'those who can't teach train the teachers'. As a result, under the direction of a succession of secretaries of state for education, regulations were introduced insisting on extensive periods of school practice on university courses (up to 24 weeks of a 36-week PGCE) or alternatively allowing schools themselves to take on the training with minimal support from an institute of higher education. Ofsted began to inspect courses and to ensure that the minutiae of government requirements were met.

My own view of these developments, on the basis of a long career in teacher training in the late twentieth century, is that actual *training* for classroom work has improved dramatically – but at the expense of an *education* in education. I believe both are needed. My worry is that teachers are being trained as technicians, skilled operators within the constraints of a curriculum and pedagogy determined by others – but not as educators able to think for themselves as to what is best for their pupils.

So, what preparation should there be for those who will teach young people for 'when the oil runs out'?

Postgraduate certificates for all

I would sweep away all of the current programmes and replace them with a postgraduate course, in a university, lasting a year and a half, starting in January.

The preliminary degree course in one or more academic or vocational disciplines is important because it gives the graduate a footing in the world of knowledge and the justifiable self-esteem that that generates. It should be seen as the entry ticket to 'walking tall' in society – not the meal ticket for future high earnings. For those intending to be primary school teachers I am not sure that the actual subject of study matters, since these teachers inevitably have to be generalists. But for intending secondary teachers, the first degree needs to cover the subject, or subjects, to be taught.

After graduation from the degree course I want the intending teacher to have a gap of at least half a year for travel (by bike, bus or train rather than aeroplane) or for work (on a farm or in a factory rather than office-based), in order to broaden experience of the world at large. It is an important step towards the maturity that young teachers need to gain.

The postgraduate course should have four elements:

- a strong school focus embracing the best of today's training, with about half of the time spent in a number of schools;
- a strong element of pedagogic theory – on a range of relevant subjects for primary teachers, and on the degree subject for secondary students, with additional studies on the development of English – i.e. on reading, writing, speaking and listening;
- a good grounding in educational theory – child development, psychology, history of education and philosophy of education;
- coverage of environmental futures.

'Embracing the best of today's training' and 'pedagogic theory' have their dangers. Students need to learn all they can about how teachers work. They must learn how to promote reading, writing, speaking and listening; how to run classroom discussions and handle open-ended questioning; how to maintain order and good discipline; how to relate to parents; how to assess children's progress and master the important pedagogic skills of assessment for learning. They should gain extensive experience of working with young people in different schools and develop thorough self-confidence. But they should also realise that the formalised planning and lesson structure required of all teachers today is not the only way to teach. Books like Sybil Marshall's *An Experiment in Education* (1963) and Brown and Precious's *The Integrated Day in the Primary Classroom* (1968) should be on the reading list for intending primary school teachers in order to show what those who were excellent teachers were achieving in the informal classrooms of the 1960s.

All that I want to say about a 'good grounding in educational theory' is that it should be taught through extensive reading by students and by regular writing of short essays presented in seminars and small-group or individual tutorials, with very few lectures and no rote-learning examinations. The educational ideas of thinkers like Dewey, Whitehead, Piaget, Bloom, Bruner, Hirst, Phenix, Schwab, Kelly, Pring, Black, Elliott, Stenhouse, Rudduck and others should be available for students to read and to argue about, to help them make up their own minds as to what education is about.

Tutors must engage with the thinking of their students and give substantial feedback on their endeavours. The aim here is to create educators who can explore the 'worthwhile' of education, not to train technicians who expect to be *told* what is 'worthwhile'.

But what of the fourth element?

Environmental futures

This is virgin territory. It is why the course needs to be longer than the traditional PGCE. It is the education for creating sustainable living that is discussed in the previous chapter. It comes in several parts.

1. 'Worthwhile survival'

Essentially, this part of the course needs to be based on the ideas of Chapter 9: learning for when the oil runs out. It is about bringing together the development of cognitive skills, environmental and social sensitivities, civic skills, environmental understanding, convivial values, critical reflection on society's actions, and empowerment to act in order to be able to take steps to achieve a sustainable way of life.

2. Books for reading, discussing, writing about

Awareness arises from extensive reading. These are some of the books that I would recommend; others would no doubt exclude some of the following and add alternatives. The first four had a profound effect on thinking around the world in the 1970s and 1980s. They led me to a personal synthesis of ideas based on the idea of conviviality. That they were all published in the years 1972–1973 may be an artefact of my choice, but I think it more likely that it is a reflection of the fact that, a quarter of a century after the end of World War II, when industrial reconstruction had repaired many of the ravages of war, people were beginning to ask the philosophical question, 'Where is this taking us?' Although a number of significant books were published in subsequent years, I have chosen to jump from there to some publications of the twenty-first century.

Blueprint for Survival, by E. Goldsmith, R. Allen, M. Allaby, J. Davoll and S. Lawrence (1972), carried the devastating message that 'the principal defect of the industrial way of life with its ethos of expansion is that it is not sustainable'. It focused on industrial societies and provided, as its title implied, a plan for making developed societies sustainable. It was widely read and then totally ignored.

The Limits to Growth, by D.H. Meadows, D.L. Meadows, J. Randers and W.W. Behrens, from the Club of Rome (1972), had a similar message – that 'the most probable result [of current growth trends] will be a rather sudden and uncontrollable decline in both population and industrial capacity'. Unlike the first book, it was based on computer analyses of complex world systems. It was criticised when the 'uncontrollable decline' hadn't happened. But although they had the time scale wrong, the 'probable result' still lies ahead.

Both of these books were concerned with population growth, economic growth, disruption of ecological systems and exhaustion of natural resources. The latter was widely read and certainly was the more criticised of the two because its computer-based scenarios were more easily challenged than the qualitative descriptions of *Blueprint*. There was a tendency for scientists to support the doom-laden predictions without challenge, for economists to oppose them without recognising their significance, and for policy-makers to treat them as a seven-day wonder and then forgot them. Today, industrial decline is seen in terms of economic problems rather than physical limits, there is less focus on population growth, there are similar concerns about disruption of ecological systems, and there is grave concern about something which was known about back then but hadn't yet surfaced significantly – climate change through global warming.

Small is Beautiful, by E.F. Schumacher (1973), soon became a catchphrase on the lips of many who had neither read the book nor reflected on the issues which Schumacher tackled. Yet thousands did read it and welcomed the introduction of moral arguments into debate about the economics of the future. His essay on 'Buddhist economics' contains one of the most magnificent paragraphs ever written. I have taken the liberty of de-gendering the original.

> The Buddhist point of view takes the function of work to be at least threefold: to give all people a chance to utilise and develop their faculties; to enable them to overcome their ego-centredness by joining with other people in a common task; and to bring forth the goods and services needed for a becoming existence... To organise work in such a manner that it becomes meaningless, boring, stultifying, or nerve-racking for the worker would be little short of criminal; it would indicate a greater concern with goods than with people, an evil lack of compassion and a soul-destroying degree of attachment to the most primitive side of this worldly existence. Equally, to strive for leisure as an alternative to work would be

166

considered a complete misunderstanding of one of the basic truths of human existence, namely that work and leisure are complementary parts of the same living process and cannot be separated without destroying the joy of work and the bliss of leisure.

Tools for Conviviality, by Ivan Illich (1973), starkly demonstrated the way in which people are losing their autonomy as an inevitable consequence of the way we allow technology to develop. It could provide a sharp challenge to those who implement managerialist approaches in the public services, but sadly, few of today's leaders have even heard of Illich. In developing the concept of conviviality as presented in this book, I took Illich's word and extended its meaning to embrace the moral concepts of Schumacher and, placing it in the global context of both *Blueprint for Survival* and *The Limits to Growth*, expressed it as a human and joyful consequence of seeking harmony with others, with the natural and cultural environments, and with oneself.

No Nonsense Guide to Globalization, by Wayne Ellwood (2001), opened my eyes to the notion that economic poverty around the globe is as big a problem facing the world as ecological degradation. He wrote:

> Corporate-led globalization is a juggernaut, driven by greed and notions of economic efficiency, which is radically altering social relationships, impoverishing millions of fellow humans, stripping age-old cultures of their self-identity and threatening the environmental health of the Earth.

But he remains an optimist by noting that this is not inevitable: global systems are human-made. He says that there is a worldwide movement to rethink globalisation, and that day by day it grows stronger. And he sees this movement as premised on a central truth:

> The only way to convince states to act in the interests of their people is to construct a system that will put humans back in control at the centre of economic activity.

The Fourth Pillar of Sustainability, by Jon Hawkes (2001), links culture with ecological, social and economic sustainability and argues that any planning process of government should pass through a framework of questions arising from all four of these 'pillars'. He believes that it is local government in direct interaction with its communities that should take the lead in striving for a sustainable society. He gives the valuable definition of 'culture' which I have used in Chapter 2.

Sustainable Education: Re-visioning Learning and Change, by Stephen Sterling (2001). His argument is that the difference between a sustainable future (which he seeks) and a chaotic future (which he considers we are fast heading towards) is transformative learning based on an ecological, participative world view in which change in education and change in society interact and support each other.

The Spirit Level: Why More Equal Societies Almost Always Do Better, by Richard Wilkinson and Kate Pickett (2009). This I hold to be one of the most significant political books of this century so far. It explores the contradiction between the material success of many industrial countries and their social failings – and shows how inequalities between rich and poor exacerbate social problems. The Nordic countries, with less inequality, have fewer social problems than many other industrial countries. In their final chapter (pp. 264–265), they write:

We hope we have shown that there is a better society to be won: a more equal society in which we regain a sense of community, in which we overcome the threat of global warming, in which we own and control our work democratically as part of a community of colleagues, and share in the benefits of a growing non-monetarised sector of the economy... [I]t falls to our generation to make one of the biggest transformations in human history. We have seen that the rich countries have got to the end of the really important contributions which economic growth can make to the quality of life and also that our future lies in improving the quality of the social environment in our societies.

All Consuming, by Neal Lawson (2009). 'Turbo-consumption' is the name that Lawson gives to current household and family expenditure. He describes how and why our consumption of goods and services has accelerated, and sees this as the human cause of global warming and climate change. He argues for a steady state economy based on a minimum wage, and citizen's income and an end to turbo-consumerism.

Government action is required to establish a post-consumer world. First, the state can stop harmful consumer practices by restricting advertising, taxing luxury goods and rationing scarce resources. Second, it can help foster good buying behaviour and activity by making ethical shopping and recycling easier. Finally, through our democracy, we can create spaces in which markets are restricted and effectively regulated, so we can be citizens, not just consumers, to help us forge more durable and satisfying identities as workers while providing us with the time and money to live more autonomous lives.

Dark Mountain, edited by Paul Kingsnorth and Dougald Hine (2010) is a collection of essays, fiction, poetry, conversations and images which I quoted from earlier. It developed from *Uncivilisation,* a manifesto written by the editors, which said:

> It's time to stop pretending our current way of living can be made 'sustainable'; that 'saving' the planet has become a bad joke; that we are entering an age of mass disruption, and our task is to live through it as best we can; that how good or bad a job we make of this is as much down to the stories we tell ourselves, our ways of seeing the world, as it is to the technologies or international treaties on which the environmental movement has pinned its hopes.

3. Working with children outside school

When I was a teacher-training tutor at Nottingham Trent, each year we took our first-year students camping with local schoolchildren, staying in a field in Anglesey. We saw it as one of the more important parts of our course – for students to work with children outside school. After the camp had been running for a few years, in 1981 I put a 'diary' article in the *Times Higher Education Supplement* about it. These are a few extracts:

> **Thursday:** Arrived at the campsite at Dulas, Anglesey. There are 41 BEd students (primary generalist and mental handicap courses), and nine tutors. Tomorrow, 70 children will arrive with seven teachers; they come from four Nottingham primary schools, and from an ESN(M) and an ESN(S) school. In all, 127 people under canvas, the schools in one field and the polytechnic in another.

Friday: In the CNAA course document, the purpose is described as 'experience of working with children in an environment other than school' ... We are in 12 domestic groups for cooking and eating. Each has a 10ft x 10ft tent with trestle table, trestle seats and gas cookers. Pete drilled us all on fire precautions, and the field is dotted with fire extinguishers.

Saturday: The Porth Wen group (seven students, 20 children, one teacher and me) met at 9.30 am in one of the marquees after heavy rain. We sat in a circle and tried to learn each other's names: most of the kids find it easy, but I am awful at it and keep making mistakes. If you don't know each other's names, how can you work together? We set off with packed lunches in two minibuses. The morning was spent exploring the brickworks. Each child had a small clipboard with a set of drawings and plans of the brickworks which we had run off on the camp hand duplicator yesterday. They had been told that parts of the building were dangerous, and that they had to look carefully at the place and note on their papers all the places that might be hazardous. After lunch it was raining, so we sat in a circle inside one of the kilns and talked about the morning's work. The acoustics of this domed building were excellent. We discussed brick-making, and I gave a short history of the site. There was a singsong until the rain stopped. We walked to Hell's Mouth. It is a most beautiful stretch of coastline, with every shade of green and brown in the vegetation and grey in the rock, plus patches of purple heather. Again it rained, but the kids never grumbled. Some of them still had energy for running up rocky mounts and hurling stones into the sea. When we got back to the minibuses, I was relieved to count 29 people again. We returned to camp and I collected a large pile of wet jeans to take to the local launderette...

Friday: Strike camp. Thank goodness for sunshine. It has been a tremendous camp. It isn't really about children and fieldwork: it's about people living together in an unfamiliar setting, relating to strangers of different ages and different abilities, making friendships, talking and thinking together, surviving under adverse weather conditions and enjoying it. If education is learning about life, this camp has been good education for everybody – children, students, teachers and tutors.

I see this kind of activity as an essential part of the new teacher training. It should be coupled with other countryside events. When my wife was a primary head teacher, she and I for several years accompanied parties of 7–8-year-olds for three-night visits to youth hostels in Derbyshire. I remember the surprise on one lad's face when he realised that the thing standing on four legs in a corner of a field was a cow. We visited the plague village of Eyam and, as part of telling the heroic story of the villagers, danced 'Ring-a-ring of roses' on the village green. More than the value of the social experience of being away from home for a few days was the experience of education outside the school classroom: of meeting nature first-hand – walking breathlessly up hills, avoiding sheep dung while walking across fields, hearing rooks in the tree-tops, learning that nettles sting if touched, feeling the wind and sometimes the rain.

4. Activities that demonstrate the practicality of sustainable living
Suppose that every student is given a patch of land, an allotment, gardening tools and seeds, and required to grow sufficient

vegetables to (hopefully) feed several people during the coming year. There are many accounts of how to do this. My favourite is the book by John Seymour, *The Complete Book of Self-Sufficiency* (1976), which gives a detailed account of how a family could live comfortably on one acre of 'good well-drained' land. He was a pioneer of convivial living, and says this in his book concerning the way towards self-sufficiency:

> It is going forward to a new and better sort of life, a life which is more fun than the over-specialized round of office or factory, a life that brings challenge and the use of daily initiative back to work, and variety, and occasional great success and occasional abysmal failure. It means the acceptance of complete responsibility for what you do or what you do not do, and one of its greatest rewards is the joy that comes from seeing each job right through – from sowing your own wheat to eating your own bread, from planting a field of pig food to slicing a side of bacon.
>
> Self-sufficiency does not mean 'going back' to the acceptance of a lower standard of living. On the contrary, it is the striving for a higher standard of living, for food which is fresh and organically grown and good, for the good life in pleasant surroundings, for the health of body and peace of mind which comes with hard varied work in the open air, and for the satisfaction that comes from doing difficult and intricate jobs well and successfully.

I am not suggesting that this is a model for everyone's future. Certainly only a small section of the population is likely to choose homestead living along the lines suggested by John Seymour. His enthusiasm has to be moderated by the recognition that it is much harder for a family to aim for family self-sufficiency than for a nation to aim at national self-sufficiency.

Seymour's way of life demands personal resilience and family coherence, as well as extensive knowledge of small-scale farming practice. But as an idea for students to try to emulate for one year, it could have a profound impact on their future teaching. In particular, if the going gets really tough in, say, thirty years' time and communities need to be at least partly self-sufficient, the teacher trained on this programme will be able to take a leading part in helping the community to grow its own produce.

By starting the 18-month course in January, students could work up their patch in the first spring and harvest their crops in the summer and autumn.

A sad and polemical footnote: GOVErnment ideas

This is unashamedly an outspoken book, and so it will be no surprise to the reader that I am appalled at the ideas about teacher education developed in November 2010 by Michael Gove, Secretary of State for Education.

His aim is to move the preparation of teachers away from universities and more into classroom-based training. It would mean that one in every three primary schools would permanently have one would-be teacher in training on its staff – a phenomenal burden on many schools. Gove describes teaching as a craft, and wants new recruits to learn everything from hands-on experience in classrooms, guided by good teachers. If the world were static that might suffice, but it is not. Of course would-be teachers require extensive experience of schools, but so much more is involved, including a theoretical input to underpin the development of the individual, the school and the national system.

Why Gove denigrated the university departments of education is not clear, but many may wonder why he trotted the globe

– to Sweden, the USA, China and South Korea, among other countries – looking for 'good' ideas, and yet ignored the significant research into pedagogy carried out by some of our English academics. It is an extraordinary feature of our governmental system that someone with a sharp mind but little experience of education is allowed to exercise such dictatorial power. Democracy should demand that government ministers listen before they act – to those with relevant understanding: heads and teachers, professional associations, and academic researchers.

It should be remembered that in 1972, when Margaret Thatcher was Secretary of State for Education, she commissioned a seven-member team, led by the Vice Chancellor of York University and former High Master of Manchester Grammar School (Lord James), to enquire into the present arrangements for the education, training and probation of teachers in England and Wales, and in particular to examine what should be the content and organisation of courses to be provided (and related matters). They reported after a year's deliberations. They took evidence from 37 organisations and interviewed 23 people, and the report covered 128 pages. In the event only some of its suggestions were implemented, and sadly the proposals for in-service education, while generally welcomed, were not implemented because of economic problems in the 1970s.

Why didn't Mr Gove set up a similar enquiry before acting with such haste? Why did he take so much on his own shoulders? How did he get a mandate to act in this way? What is wrong with our political system that a minister is allowed to get away with being in such a hurry?

Endnote:

Educating the Next Generation for the Inevitable Crisis

Figure 5 illustrates the way in which the various ideas put forward in this book, which to some may seem a curious medley, actually are all essential if teachers are to be able to educate the next generation in ways which will equip them to cope with the inevitable ecological/economic crisis that will hit our society during their lifetime.

The beginning may be the most difficult stage: recognition of the inevitability of the coming of a society-disrupting crisis. It is not easy to believe that the shock caused to our way of living by the casino-banking/sub-prime-mortgage crisis of 2008–2010 will be tiny compared with what will happen in the UK when oil supply peaks and rapidly declines, causing personal and freight transport to become prohibitively expensive. Or when climate change causes dramatic changes to our agriculture, with massive food and water shortages, or when other catastrophes – as yet unknown – arise from our turbo-consumerist obsession with economic growth.

Once the impending crisis is recognised as inevitable, it points to the urgent need for education. Adult education through the media for the present electorate, and school education for the next generation.

Yes, reform of the national newspapers: replacing the rapacious press barons by not-for-profit trusts. These trusts should recognise that, in addition to their newspapers' reporting of popular culture, celebrity scandals and sports events, they should also act as an educative force which keeps the nation informed about the perils ahead and gives government ministers ample opportunity to explain, and opposition spokesmen the chance to question, the decisions they are taking to avert these perils.

Some major decisions have to be made. The first of these must be to reduce the vast disparity in incomes in our society – the gross inequality which has a strong bearing on social and health problems. The suggestions in Chapter 1 are that a maximum wage and citizen's income be introduced. Like other proposals here, they depend upon the press giving a fair and balanced hearing to them, not just denigration by the capitalist press barons – who own most of our papers – and their compliant editors.

In parallel to these changes, there must be a transfer of control of education from government to collegially operating schools. This will be aided if there is a widespread recognition (explained by an unbiased press) that schooling is not simply a preparation for working life, but should be based on understandings of nurture, culture and survival. I argue that Occam's razor should be applied to Sats, Ofsted and league tables, and that in their place a more effective accountability system should be developed – bottom-up, from school self-evaluation and governors' reports, not top-down from government via Ofsted. Coupled with this is the expectation that every school should become a good school, arising from collegial organisation.

With the reduction in inequality it should be easier to see

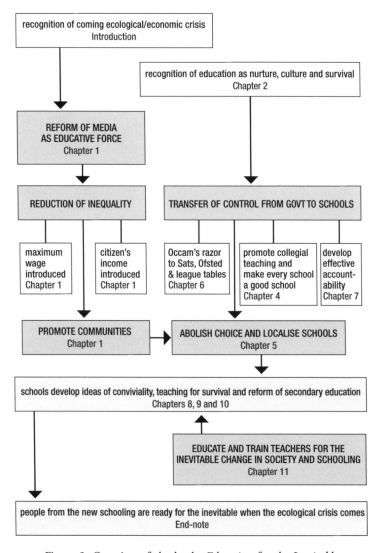

Figure 5. Overview of the book: *Educating for the Inevitable*

communities becoming stronger, and this links to the idea that choice of schools should be abolished, with all children going to their local schools within firm catchment areas. But choice can only be ruled out when every school is a good school and is perceived as such by the local community. Local schools will help build the strong communities that will be needed when the oil begins to run out and personal transport becomes very expensive.

By this stage we can hope that schools have begun to recognise the importance of teaching for the inevitable crisis and will adopt ideas about conviviality and survival and relate these to ways of rethinking the secondary school curriculum. Likewise, it will be important that the education and training of teachers for work in schools is in accord with ideas of what the future may hold. I have suggested a one-and-a-half-year postgraduate course for every teacher, with plenty of experience in classrooms.

So, my hope is that if these ideas are implemented, the people who will be in their mature years in twenty, thirty and forty years' time will have had a schooling that has prepared them to think effectively about responding to whatever ecological and economic crises hit their society. They are my grandchildren's generation. I shall not live to see what happens, but I trust they will be prepared, and will act wisely and convivially.

Index